WIN AT ROULETTE

GORDON CROMWELL

OLDCASTLE BOOKS

1990

Oldcastle Books Ltd
18 Coleswood Road
Harpenden, Herts AL5 1EQ

Copyright © Gordon Cromwell 1990

All rights reserved. No part of this book may be reproduced,
stored in a retrieval system, or transmitted in any form,
or by any means, electronic, mechanical, photocopying,
recording or otherwise, without the written permission
of the publishers.

British Library Cataloguing in Publication Data — record
available for Win at Roulette

ISBN 0 948353 78 3

9 8 7 6 5 4 3 2 1

Printed by The Guernsey Press Co. Ltd.,
Guernsey, Channel Islands.

CONTENTS

Introduction		1
Chapter 1	Facing the Odds	5
Chapter 2	Roulette -- Spinning to Disaster?	16
Chapter 3	Staking Highlighted	26
Chapter 4	Profiting Even from the Even Chances	35
Chapter 5	Finding Favourable Foursomes	41
Chapter 6	Occupational Therapy at 2/1	45
Chapter 7	Sleeping Partners	49
Chapter 8	The Persistent or "Hot" Numbers	53
Chapter 9	The "Silly" System	57
Chapter 10	Managing Your Money	62
Chapter 11	Crooked Wheel? Forget It!	67
Chapter 12	Betting Strategy Summarised as Question and Answer	71
Appendix 1	Playing a Specimen Session	73
Appendix 2	A Session from Published Spins	77
Appendix 3	Keeping Track of Wins and Losses	81
Index		83

WIN AT ROULETTE

INTRODUCTION

"The casino always wins."

If you failed to believe that, whether from general knowledge, bitter experience, or mathematical appreciation, you might expect to be charged with having no common sense. So you are right to be sceptical of any contrary claim. The author makes exactly such a contrary claim in these words: THERE ARE WAYS, IN A SERIES OF SHORT-TERM OPERATIONS, BY WHICH MONEY CAN BE WON FROM A CASINO.

If you are one of the many people who has never been into a casino, what sort of picture does the word conjure up? Is it somewhere where, having gambled away his all, the ruined punter shoots himself on the balcony? You might remember that the unequalled "Sergeant Bilko" partly fooled the casino management into reimbursing him his losses to avoid the scandal of an apparently threatened suicide, but that as so often happened to him in those plot-packed short films, he was later found out when trying to repeat the hoax. Even today, isn't it likely that the first reaction to "casino" in anyone's mind is the instant thought of Monte Carlo?

You may never have heard of Charles Wells, but as we are thinking about betting, I'll bet you know the song he inspired. It was of course, "The Man Who Broke the Bank at Monte Carlo." In the summer of 1891, with the very large sum of £4,000 in his pocket, he first went to the casino. When he left, he was richer by 250,000 francs, and had caused a sensation. Breaking the bank didn't mean breaking the casino, but it had meant that the croupier's "till" of one hundred-thousand francs had gone and had to be replenished.

Charles Wells hadn't finished with the casino. He kept on playing throughout that summer and his phenomenal luck stayed with him so that he was able to break the bank a number of times. He even won by tripling bets, that is, allowing his wins to stay on for two further spins, an extremely optimistic, illogical and hazardous way of playing. Inevitably he attracted a very great deal of publicity, to say nothing of begging demands and pleas for the secret of his systematic success. He gave nothing away beyond the advice to watch how he played. It seems that nobody became any the wiser doing that.

One day he lost over a hundred-thousand francs before recovering it and an additional thirty-thousand. Later in the year he left Monte Carlo, threatening to return to play them out of business. The founder, Monsieur Francois Blan, was said to have predicted that, "He who breaks the bank today will be broken by the bank tomorrow." Wells had reputedly been in great financial difficulty in England, even to the extent of risking imprisonment for fraud.

He returned in 1892 in a luxury yacht. The casino directors were pleased, confident that their wheels would in the end defeat any gambler. By the time he had broken the bank six more times, they were less happy, but his luck did turn, and after successive bad losses, he began to play the maximum of twelve-thousand francs on every bet. The wheel at last beat him, but there was far worse to come. It transpired that he had spent his immense winnings of the previous year, had fraudulently obtained the second year's capital and was sentenced at the Old Bailey to a long term of penal servitude. This didn't deter him from a future life of fraud which earned him a prison sentence in France. He died in England in 1922.

Charles Wells claimed in later years that there was no secret plan to reveal. He had used a number of different "systems" but it was nothing but luck which had been responsible for his monumental total of winnings. If it was, one can only marvel at that absolutely monumental luck, and regret its wanton destruction.

That rather sad but cautionary tale shouldn't in any way lead you to think that a casino is packed with criminal types. In any case, what is a criminal type? You might just as easily have one sitting opposite you in a train and have no reason to identify him as such. As for Mr. Wells, "Surely," we can ask ourselves, "someone would have to be very weak and entirely unthinking to give back everything from even a single large win?" The need to ask the question probably shows one reason why the casino wins. Undeniably, the casino in its total transactions with all its patrons *is* the winner. Yet, honest sceptic, why does the management of a casino find it necessary or prudent occasionally to ban a punter for winning consistently? Whether they would like to admit such a thing publicly is doubtful, but then if you have been clever enough to warrant receiving their letter terminating your membership, no reference need be made to your "sin" in beating the odds. "The Committee regrets..." is all the explanation their rules require them to offer.

Members are banned from casinos for bad behaviour, making a nuisance of themselves, perhaps for purloining another punter's cash chips, (and being found out), or simply because the watchdog saw that someone had discovered a way of becoming more than just a "lucky punter."

Casinos love lucky punters. Envious but encouraged eyes watch as stacks of winning chips are pushed towards those happy people. When a lucky punter's luck changes, the croupier or "dealer" is there to claw back all those winning chips -- and more besides, as they did from Charles Wells. Human nature is so frail that a good win often nullifies logical thinking.

When you have learnt how to take advantage of the short-term trends which are constantly available for discovery, you might even be well advised to operate at two or more different casinos, if that is possible. Remember, you will have lifted yourself out of the class of lucky punter into that of

KNOWLEDGEABLE PUNTER". Now, instead of loving you, the casino will be poised to hate you. And once it hates you, there's a good chance that your membership will be at risk. Could you ask for a better way to earn such a testimonial?

Arithmetic cannot be divorced from any form of gambling, therefore no apology is offered for examining and demonstrating what odds are ranged against optimistic punters in the most usual fields of betting. Anyone thinking of Roulette, and for that matter, Blackjack, as nothing but games of chance, overlooks a most significant mathematical aspect of those games. The 2.7% advantage to the house at Roulette is obvious, based as it is on the payment of 35/1 for the 36/1 chance the punter takes when selecting and backing the winning number.

In passing, it can be noted that every chance between the player and dealer at Blackjack is represented by the percentage performance of an ordinary pack of fifty-two playing cards. It might almost call for an apology to state the obvious fact that on average you would expect to be dealt every named card in the pack for every 52 cards received; or that you would have <u>an</u> ace for every 13 cards dealt to you -- there being four aces in each pack. Averages of course emerge from the longer term performances of whatever elements one is considering.

Although the punter's handicap at Roulette is no more than 2.7%, (and at Blackjack <u>should</u> be almost as low as a third of that), it is the carefree attitude of the players themselves which allows the Gaming Board to publish figures showing that the U.K. casinos are able to retain for themselves £20 of every £100 exchanged for chips. The description "carefree" covers all the false optimism, the superstition, the compulsive gambling, and, worst of all, the almost total ignorance of the extent to which mathematics governs casino games.

This insistence on the necessity to take account of arithmetic in no way implies that in order to win, you would be involved in abstruse calculations. The various profitable methods recommended take care of the arithmetic, and the player is called on for nothing more complicated than adding or subtracting wins and losses, and being able to keep an eye on the overall money total. It surely isn't unreasonable to expect you to know when you are winning, when to pocket those winnings, or when to withdraw your custom, even though temporarily, to avoid further loss.

Roulette produces arithmetical behaviour-patterns which are quite easily identifiable and can be made to work for the benefit of the player. This is not to say that if you back a number for 111 spins you are guaranteed even one of your expected three winners in that time. But then, one of the earliest lessons prohibits the blind "chasing" of numbers. You must never back a number without a good reason for doing so, and that good reason must be unearthed from short-term arithmetic as distinct from that of the long term. Against infinity, yours is a doomed cause. To the casino, infinity is a delight.

This book realistically warns of the dangers of opposing

the odds inherent in gambling and then, after examining the particular problems attaching to Roulette, sets out precisely how, with patience and discipline, you may expect to win money from casinos and to do it without impossibly large capital risks. Obviously enough, risk can never be eliminated from gambling. Finally, you are advised how best to stay ahead of the game once you have won some of "their" money and converted it into "your" money.

CHAPTER 1

FACING THE ODDS

If someone claims that it is possible to win from a casino and not only to win but to stay a winner, when everyone knows that it is the casinos which always win, you are entitled to look askance. Because this is a claim that is being made, let's start by briefly staring gambling straight in the eye. There is no better way of preparing for a fight than assessing the strength of your opponent. Hence the high priority given to reconnaissance by armed forces. Make no mistake, gambling is a battle and yours certainly is the weaker army. In the end, whether you win or lose will depend on the degree to which you exploit the enemy's weakness rather than the throwing of everything against his known strength. The Army defines this principle as reinforcing success.

Essentially, gambling is the opposition of mathematical odds which are against you and must in the long term prevail. If you had four equal chances of winning but were paid only twice your stake for every time you won; despite retaining your winning stake, as each success would be balanced by three losses, you would finish by losing three stakes and winning two stakes for every attempt made. Just as a moderate Second Division football team drawn against a highly-rated First Division team playing before its own supporters could expect to lose far more often than it won, so will a punter lose if he constantly bets against arithmetic.

If from your four winning chances you were paid three times your stakes for your wins the final result would be a draw. You would finish all square. The catch is that you won't find anyone who would pay to set up a business which could expect only to break even on its turnover.

It follows that the whole gaming industry is based on an arithmetical certainty that the punter will be offered less than the true odds relating to any betting situation. I suppose there's hardly a better way of warning you off gambling! Yet if you won your first four bets at those odds of 2/1, you might pocket the eight units, and run. Or, if you chose to go on betting and lost six of those eight units, you could still run with the remaining two. Yes, and you would have beaten the odds. That is the rock on which successful betting may be built, namely the advantage to be taken from short-term winning positions against the long-term certainty of loss. "Right," you say. "What's the problem? I shall stop every time I have a winner."

I'm sorry, misguided punter, but that won't do at all. I know how popular it is for you to be advised to stop at a win. The terrible weakness about it is that, although surely it wouldn't be your intention, you'd so organise your betting that you'd have to keep on doing it while you were losing. Away goes your money, time after time, and then at last you win some of it back, and you STOP. I'm not specifically advising it, but wouldn't it be infinitely more sensible if you went on betting for as long as winners were coming up and then stopped at your first, (or at worst, second), loss? However you answer this, it cannot be right to order yourself to suffer the misery of all the losing runs you fall into, but not once, ever, allow the sunshine of a winning run to warm your heart.

HORSE SENSE

In gambling there is said to be no such thing as a certainty. On the other hand you can probably think of many circumstances which would appear to be so one-sided that no layer would offer you odds to bet on. A Derby winner running against the milkman's horse would be an absurdly contrived "certainty" to win -- unless of course the jockey fell off, or he or the horse had a heart attack, or the horse stumbled over an anachronistic suffragette. A cruel coincidence? Of course. Impossible? Not if the unbelievable match were set up.

I remember that very many years ago having read that professional backers often took more than one horse in a race to make winning more likely, I backed three horses in a steeplechase at Sandown Park. The odds were such that if any of the three won I should make a satisfactory profit. On approaching the last turn before the home run my three animals were galloping strongly in line, a very long way in front of the rest of the field. Now I could stand and cheer whichever of the three lasted best up the hill. Good horses rarely fall, and I had three good ones on my side. For once it was quite an experience to know that it didn't matter which one won. At the bottom fence they all took off together. The outside horse jumped right across the other two and one, if not both, went over the rail into the centre of the course. The precise details don't matter because in any case all three were out of the race. The warning is that your certainty is never that until the cash is in your hand.

Betting on horses is complicated by the fact that even chances are almost never involved. I don't mean that no even money prices are offered but that chances are neither easy to evaluate nor are genuinely even. Form, the historical and statistical report on what a horse has previously achieved, is by no means always a guarantee of a repeat performance. There is a whole list of different conditions which might obstruct such a happy result; differently shaped courses both laterally and vertically, the inclusion of horses of varying ages and sexes, changed jockeys, underfoot conditions made softer or harder by rain or sun, more or less weight to be carried, and the imponderable of whether a horse feels sufficiently well or temperamentally content to run to its best potential -- and always provided that human agency, whether trainer, jockey or drug administrator doesn't intervene to the detriment of that previous form.

The available odds on any race therefore depend on the

majority opinion about each horse's ability but are effectively
restricted by bookmakers' ever increasing greed, and reduced by
the Government's imposition of Betting Tax. Years ago when the
Irish equipped wonderful hospitals from the proceeds of official
sweepstakes on certain British races, the holy and hypocritical
caucuses were not only instrumental in largely preventing the
sales of those tickets to the British, but blocked the sort of
scheme which surely would have done infinitely more good than
harm to the nation as a whole. The implication was that it would
have been as immoral to profit from gambling, (however pure the
cause), as it might have been to benefit from the proceeds of
prostitution. People needed to be protected from themselves.
Do-gooders were doing their worst.

Some years later, still without a national lottery or even
a national football pool, (the "pools" looking like the worst
value of all to the punter), the keepers of the official conscience persuaded themselves that it was acceptable to demand
extra money from gambling, (no cries of "shame"?), in the form
of a Tax on betting. As bookmakers were made responsible for
collecting this money, they soon decided to add a fraction for
themselves -- if 25% rates a "fraction". At present, should you
miraculously have £10 on each of ten successive winners, and
place your bets in a betting shop, you forfeit, regardless of
the prices of the winners, £10 from those stakes, (the majority
of course going to the Government), plus a further 10% from your
total winnings; again with 8% reserved for the Treasury.

We may speculate on the thinking behind this moral
turnabout. Was the Tax intended to discourage gambling? Whose
conscience was appeased in order that the Government should now
be able to live in part on these immoral earnings? Was it just a
juicy grabbing of more easy money? It is doubtful that tobacco
tax has saved many lives. It has been pointed out that but for
gambling, there would be no horse racing, and surely that would
never do. Apart from being a fact of life, it is a vast
industry, the employer of a large workforce -- and obviously as
a result, was already the contributor of significant Taxes.

For the punter, it becomes inexorably more difficult and
less worthwhile for him to wager successfully. Indeed, some
years ago a racing correspondent in the "Observer" advised his
readers to give up betting on horses but to bet on the Shares of
the bookmaking Companies.

Those who continue to bet and think it safest to follow the
majority opinion, that is to say the majority opinion in terms
of the most money, will go for favourites. These do give some
credence to the existence of "form" because they manage to win
rather more than one race in four, however, their prices might
be as high as 5/1 or as low as 1/5, and on average are
uncomfortably mean. Not everyone can afford to travel to a
racecourse in order to bet, although at the present time that
would eliminate the Tax deductions, but the punter who fancies a
horse at a particular price, often does well to accept that
price as soon as it is on offer. Otherwise, if it is a horse
which is being backed in any way heavily in the betting-shops
around the country, the "big" bookmakers are going to siphon

considerable money back to the course to ensure that if the horse wins, the price will be reduced to the level that won't do much harm to them. The result of this calculated interference is that the starting price doesn't reflect the higher level at which the course bookmakers would have been willing to trade.

The punter, always faced with arithmetic, resorts to some doubtful remedies including the attempt to win a fixed amount together with any previous losses, and the horror of planning to double his stakes until a winner is found, (he hopes!), because surely one favourite must win in the afternoon? This matter of staking, including the avoidance of some suicidal staking methods, is relevant to all types of gaming, and will be dealt with in its turn.

You might improve your chances by specialising in certain types of races; non-handicaps for example; and particularly by two-year-olds recording fast times, but the form is "exposed" and bookmakers don't give money away. So £100 on your certainty at odds of 1/2 in a betting shop would see your basic return of £150 reduced by Tax to £135. How often are you going to risk £100 for a possible gain of £35? And if you were going to lay out £5 or £10, surely you would forget it as worthless.

Up to about the middle nineteen-sixties and certainly before that, there were people, call them professional backers if you like, who won money mostly by level-stake betting on carefully selected form horses. A few made very considerable yearly sums. One or two sold their expertise as occasional selections and undoubtedly made it possible for the buyers to win. The backlash was that as soon as these advisers showed themselves to be consistently successful, the bookmakers also became buyers and immediately reduced the prices offered against such selections. As these had been chosen with a view to the likely value obtainable, the whole exercise was weakened.

It is now widely accepted that those favourable conditions have vanished, no doubt permanently, and if the professional backer is helpless, how can you, ordinary punter, expect a profit? You feel driven to search for longer-priced animals as a way of getting some return for your mounting outlay. Horses do win at long prices, but how do you find one? Your pin, stuck into a long list of runners, may one day provide you with a horse which is drawn too far to the outside, has never shown on a racecourse that it would be all that far in front of the milkman's horse, is ridden by an apprentice or unfashionable jockey grateful for any ride whatever.

Because of your pin, you place a bet and do cartwheels when the despised animal wins at 33/1. Then dawns the awful fear that the Stewards may call an enquiry and demand that the trainer explains how this no-hope horse has improved so dramatically. They couldn't disqualify it, could they? You know you're kidding yourself. All right, so you get your money. But how often will your pin come up with the goods? Mathematically, not often enough. There is a wide gulf between backing winners and backing enough winners at sufficient prices to enable you to bank a profit. You can often enough read the advice never to bet in handicap races. If the expert framing this kind of race does his utmost to achieve a multiple dead-heat, it stands to reason that it will not often be possible to pick out the winner, especially from a large number of runners.

One popular piece of advice is to back the favourite in maiden races. That is fine unless you happened also to read a celebrated racing journalist's opinion that you should <u>never</u> bet in three-year-old maiden races. He was convinced that over the years it would have been very bad business. Although he did not quote any figures, I take it that he found the form unreliable and that in consequence the favourites in such races were unreliable. Maiden two-year-old favourites are usually much more rewarding although the prices may not be very generous.

At the time I read the warning about three-year-old maiden races, (it was more than 20 years ago), another very well-known writer suggested that the backer should never accept a price less than 5/2 about any horse. So the immediate dilemma was whether to back short-priced favourites or wait for the few which might pass the 5/2 test. This was no problem to the man I knew who made £2,000 in each of 12 out of 13 consecutive years.

It was the mid nineteen-fifties. The man in question used to divide £2,000 into eight stakes of £250 and back horses which started at odds of 8/15 or shorter, that is to say, 1/2, 2/5, 30/100 and so on. When he had made £2,000 in any year, which sometimes happened by July, he finished serious betting for that season. As he wasn't a professional backer and had a full business life, he wrote to the systems department of one of the largest bookmaking Companies to enquire whether they would accept his bets in the form of a standing order. They kept him waiting some time before refusing his application. As this could have had nothing watever to do with adverse credit-rating, (he was much more than financially sound), or personal conduct since that was unimpeachable, the firm conclusion has to be that his system was recognised as a threat to the bookmakers' profits. After all, it was the easiest possible method to work and could have caused no operational problems to the Company.

Now, before you go running off to work this winning system which I have passed on to you in a quite unpremeditated way, please recall that I am reporting something which happend in those "Good Old Days". Let's take a fictitious but entirely possible example. We'll assume that you would suffer four losing stakes resulting in a loss of £1,000, so now in order to win the desired £2,000 you have to win £3,000. Allowing you the the slightly generous average price of 1/2 you will need to back 24 winners to achieve your target. The outlay will be £6,000 (24 at £250), and the actual return will be £9,000. Good! but you weren't able to be on the course; and you could never be at more than one course at a time in pursuit of your odds-on favourites; so away goes £900 in Betting Tax -- £25 from your stake alone for each winning bet. You see, the goalposts have been moved yet again. Possibly, because of that Tax, the system might not always yield enough winners to pay the desired net dividend.

Most bookmakers offer you the choice of paying Tax in

advance on your stake only. This means that if your bet loses, you are out of pocket by an extra 10%, but should the bet be successful, you will pay no Tax however large the win might be. For example, a £10 bet with £1 Tax paid in advance would, given a 2/1 winner, make you a £19 net profit. If you didn't pay Tax at the time of making the bet your £30 return would have £3 deducted so your equivalent profit would be only £17. The inference appears to be that if you had absolute confidence that your betting method would win on balance, you should invariably pay Tax in advance.

A final horseracing statistic which I have not personally researched was passed on to me by a man leaving the payout window with a very large bundle of banknotes. He said, "Do you know that 60% of all horses which win and run again within four days are immediate winners?" Some of them certainly have been, and the prices were greater than I should have expected.

MAD ENGLISHMEN AND DOGS

Greyhound racing, described by the late Sir Winston Churchill as animated Roulette, resembles Roulette only to the extent that both offer the backer a fixed number of choices; the 37 numbers of Roulette matched by the usual six, but sometimes eight, dogs in a race. Greyhounds, like horses, can have their good and bad days, are subject to human cheating, doping, and because there is no guiding jockey to be made accountable, the bumping and impeding of one another in their efforts to catch that improbable hare. It is usual for dogs to remain at, and become familiar with a particular track but the course is open to the elements and so is subject to change by frost, rain, snow or sunshine.

With only six choices, the betting range is naturally limited. Probably owing to the skill with which the grader or racing manager compiles the various races, the incidence of winning dog favourites approximates that of handicap races on the turf, so in proportion sets the gambler an equally difficult problem. It is worth noting at this point that although the reward for backing any number at Roulette (a 36/1 chance), is 35/1, there is no equivalent in a 37-runner horse race. In the latter, opinion might decree 4/1 against the favourite but stretch to 100/1 for one or more outsiders. This, by the way, ignores the fact that many racecourses are unable to accommodate as many as 37 runners in one contest.

Aware now, of the arithmetical habits of the bookmakers, we aren't even going to dream of a dog-race in which all six animals were quoted at 9/2, the lowest regular price which would give a return to the book from whichever one won. But if equality were needed, my guess would put the prices at 3/1. In any case I should rate it an extreme rarity for six dogs to be offered at the same price at any time in the betting. Once again, betting shops snatch Tax from winning returns, and although as you will discover, Roulette sets its own mathematical and other challenges, you do at least receive in full whatever you contrive to win. Deducting Tax would be an impossibly complicated task.

My own introduction to greyhound racing was before the age of 20 when a younger friend persuaded me to go with him to the White City in London. "There's a dog called Mick the Miller," he said. "It will win but the price won't be much." With very little money in my pocket, 2/1 didn't seem much of a price, but even as an arrant tyro I could see that "Mick" seemed to be somehow thinking his way through the tangle of dogs from which he emerged at the last bend and coasted home by two or three lengths. What a price against a dog which was already well known and on his way to becoming a phenomenon. The modern bookmaker would probably have chalked up 1/2 as the top price on offer!

The ABC of greyhound form is the electronic timing which is declared after every race or trial and is printed on the official racecard. This might, for example, show that a dog won a 500 metres race in 31.20 seconds. Another dog in the same race might be shown as having finished third in its previous race, recording a time of 31.35 seconds. All things being equal, in other words with a clear run in prospect, you might expect the first dog to be made favourite to win. Perhaps it would be. But what if that second dog had in its form line, "Bumped", "Crowded", "Impeded", or one or more such incidents in running? The vital question would be how many or how few lengths were lost by such interference. The racecard doesn't tell you, so the problem for the punter is to evaluate the distance, converted into fractions of seconds, which a dog loses by being crowded, baulked or impeded, once or more times during the running.

So perhaps this other dog was, and is, capable of beating 31.20 seconds. How does one guess whether he is on the upgrade? By his age perhaps? And then, will the potential speed of a puppy be matched by the experience of an older dog? Form students are thrown back on their own observation or on making decisions about time-allowances in order to choose between the estimated merits of any two animals. Yes, as with Roulette, it can be anybody's choice. On the other hand, you do have an option. My old friend used to say, "Does somebody order us to bet in this race? Do 'they' (the management), say we can come in only if we agree to bet in every race? Let's go and have a hot drink." Priceless advice when you are dithering between three choices on a cold winter's evening.

In what I can only describe as the good old days; which included no Betting Tax, much lower Totalisator deductions, more generous prices, and at a few tracks in London place-betting on the first three in six-dog races; a specialist paper, "The Greyhound Express", gave four form lines for every dog. You could discover how fast or slow they were from the starting traps to the first bend, where many a race is won and lost. You were given previous prices and the sort of "class" in terms of seconds in which a dog had run. The four form lines, one more than the official racecard used to print and, as far as I am aware, still print, were occasionally vital to the unearthing of a winner. The fact that the paper was allowed to close down reflected the decline in attendances at the sport. Otherwise punters would have been crazy not to keep such an invaluable source of information in being. To me, it was an irreplaceable paper, sadly mourned for many years. As the tracks are no longer on my visiting list, I cannot say whether in recent years a publisher has in any way managed to fill the void. The recent installation of television screens in the betting shops now allows a visual reading of some of the form and should at least maintain interest in this popular sport, but such luxury is restricted to a limited number of greyhound races and is available only to betting-shop patrons who can be there during the day. The evening meetings, which attracted the bulk of the attendance, have to be visited in person because except when covering evening horse racing during daylight, the betting shops are closed by Law. No doubt that will be nibbled at by the bookies.

From the ordinary present-day newspaper the backer finds almost no essential information and can do little more than take on trust the selections provided. In the majority of cases no betting forecast is printed, (beyond the bookmaker-sponsored afternoon meetings), although, generally speaking, the selection and "danger" are likely to be the first and second favourites, or at least to be with the shorter-priced returns. Missing are such obviously relevant facts as ages, times, incidents, and, for what it might be worth, the placing of the dog in its latest race. Quite often even the trap draw is not available.

It used to be an accepted statistic that an expert tipster found half the winners from his first two selections, and it is possible that it still happens. Would it help us to win? Arithmetic again. If we backed those two dogs for ten races, we should average five winners and fifteen losing stakes. If the average price of the winners came to 7/2 our return on single-unit bets of £1 would be £22.50 for an outlay of £20. Even then, you couldn't rejoice. The betting shop would deduct £2.25 in Tax, leaving you with a grand profit of 25p on an outlay of £20 over a span of ten races. Yes, and of course you're way ahead of me! An _average_ price of 7/2 is fairytale-stuff, because most of those selections would be favourite and second-favourite.

My random check at five leading London tracks yielded four wins at an average price of 1.7/1, four at 2.7/1, five at 2.05/1, five at 1.3/1 and five at 2.51/1. The results were roughly what I had expected. The prices horrified me. The meetings yielding 15 wins from 60 bets returned 45 units at the very best, and that is taking no account of Betting Tax. But then, I wasn't aiming to teach you how to win at the dogs; only, perhaps, to warn you of the pitfalls.

As a young sport, greyhound racing attracted many system-mongers who offered a variety of ways of winning. Almost without exception their methods failed to stand up to arithmetic, and people pased on dubious advice to one another, often thinking up an idea and trying it out in hard cash without any attempt to check it against past results. I had become very interested in the "new" Contract Bridge and was fascinated by the mathematical approach both to it and to dog racing.

Anti system-thinking doesn't accept that what happened in the past is any indication of what could happen in the future, yet it is fairly well established that an animal which has run a certain distance in a certain time is often capable of repeating that performance at a later date. What with track records and course records, time must always have had some bearing, greater or smaller, on the estimation of form.

One very popular belief applicable to both major sorts of betting was that you could beat the book and make an income by aiming to win a fixed sum at every meeting, the favourite normally being nominated as the crock of gold. All you needed, it was argued, was sufficient capital. Capital was hard to come by, but I soon concluded that for "sufficient" one ought to substitute "huge".

In 1930, when 10/-, (50p), a week would rent two clean unfurnished rooms in a residential area in London, two Bridge-playing friends put up some capital and went to Wembley three nights a week to win £1 and expenses by backing favourites. Whenever we asked how things were going, the reply always smugly claimed success and we began to ask less frequently. After five months or so the winnings had mounted to more than £60 and there were plans to raise the target. Had I been too cautious in thinking it was a risky plan? In any case, why not aim for two winning favourites? Two out of eight was less than the average expectation.

Came the evening when no favourite won, and £80 went back into the bookies' satchels. More than somewhat shaken, and realising that even assuming no further blank days, it would take the best part of two more months to recover even to their starting point, the partners ceased operations. It was a good decision, but what a classic example of the power of the losing run to stagger from a beaten corner and deliver a knockout blow. The modern ten-race meeting turning up a blank would probably have seen off the whole of my friends' capital.

It was my long-held belief that dog favourites were far too costly a way to try to win back earlier losses, that almost 20 years after my friends' downfall, I researched and wrote an article the second paragraph of which read, "I gave Luss Express 33/1, Castletown Plane 10/1 and Toher Dawn 10/1 all at the same meeting at Walthamstow. I also gave Ardjuin 100/6 at Harringay, and Brigadier Darkie 8/1 (a mere 8/1), at Harringay, and Hill Lass 8/1 at Stamford Bridge, and Speckled Flame 10/1 and Hidden Judy 8/1 both at the same meeting at Stamford Bridge, and Hungarian Goblet 100/8 at the White City."

Oh! no! There was no catch in it; as I clearly proved. I had taken the simplistic view that in the majority of races, the racing manager or grader had compiled a race in which he reckoned every dog had a chance. In spite of all the published statistics and written opinions, who was better placed than the grader to judge the possibilities of the dogs in the kennels? If favourites were too costly for me, how about a look at the other end of the betting-scale? There was my selection. It was the longest-priced dog in every race. You could get back a lot of your losses at 10/1 and 100/8. Only one of those at a meeting meant a level-stake profit -- and no Tax! I reduced the bets to six by eliminating the two highest class (maximum prize-money), races. Had I been trying to find a winner by studying form, I should have automatically disregarded the first graded race because, as a trainer explained to me, "They put the 'crabs' in that one." Three of those four tracks are now extinct.

FOOTBALL

Is there worse gambling-value than is offered by "the pools"? Winning the treble chance jackpot is something akin to being struck by lightning. Winning on a week when "no claims" are needed means that too many of the obvious results have come about, so nobody gets much for the trouble and outlay. If you restrict yourself to draws or aways, you will never win much unless you avoid the popular selections, for they, like favourites in racing, will be carrying the maximum money. If you take four home certainties and enter them on an aways pool, and, miraculously, they all lose at home, you are going to make yourself a very handsome dividend; that is, always provided you haven't chosen a week when most of the predictable away results have materialised, because in that case your inspired selections will be swamped by the myriads of winning lines based on the recommendations of the newspaper experts. In any case a diabolically high percentage of cash is deducted from the total pools, some for Tax, some for running costs and some as profit.

A relative of mine gave up football-pool betting and saved the equivalent stakes for the regular buying of Premium Bonds. At the present time it is claimed that a £1,000 holding gives you a statistical expectation of a prize, (of whatever value), once a year. You still have the chance of the "lightning-strike", and only inflation reduces your capital. But that same inflation no longer allows you to buy one, or even a few, Bonds, so another defensive scheme bites the dust!

The best value from football prediction **may** be found in the bookmakers' fixed odds lists. Compare them, because some are meaner than others. Choose the least number of predictions you are allowed to make and pay your money. A personal fancy is the correct scores list where you can once again bet on single matches. This type of wager was suspended for many years after a sensational claim that footballers had been bribed to ensure that a match (and possibly more than one match), ended as a specific draw or other indicated score from which those in possession of the information could frame their bets and so cheat the bookmakers. Predicting correct scores is not necessarily easy, but 1-1 turns up quite a lot in drawn matches. Home wins often end as 2-1. Both scores rate an approximate 7/1 to your money.

=========================

After the foregoing catalogue of woes, you are entitled to take a breather. You may never have intended to back a horse, a dog, or your opinion as to the outcome of one or more football matches. I know a Roulette player who says exactly that, but the game doesn't owe him anything, so he stays with it.

I have been at some pains to show optimistic punters that

challenging the mathematics of betting is a grim and dangerous pursuit. Anyone wanting to have a carefree gamble as part of an enjoyable outing has every right to risk a chosen amount of money, but I have been more concerned with the backers who keep at it, always hoping or believing that a constant profit is obtainable. Now, standing at the entrance of a casino, can you possibly expect to fare any better? I believe you can ...IF... So let's turn our attention to Roulette. That "IF" will rest almost completely with you; that is to say primarily with your application and discipline. But first, you must understand the power of the enemy, primarily based, need I add, on an arithmetical advantage of 2.7%. Betting Tax does not apply although you can suppose that the Companies responsible for the casinos pay some fancy sums in Corporation Tax.

CHAPTER 2

ROULETTE -- SPINNING TO DISASTER?

Should you think that a mere 2.7% against you is nothing to worry about, consider that one year's official Gaming Board figures for all the casinos in the United Kingdom showed that from every £100 exchanged for chips, your friendly enemy was able to bank £20 for itself. That 20% is the measure of the foolishness, foolhardiness, or ignorance of you, (us), punters.

I deliberately chose "friendly" enemy because casinos constantly maintain such an atmosphere in order to trap their unwary members somewhat as ants farm aphids for future sustenance. Let's postpone a final appreciation of all the forces ranged against us, but start with the mechanics of Roulette, so allowing me to cater for absolute beginners as well as trying to teach old dogs new tricks. The psychology can come later.

All casino gaming in the U.K. is governed by the Gaming Act, the provisions of which specifically include measures for the protection of the players. You cannot, as in many other countries, walk into a casino at any time and take part in play. You must first identify yourself, pay a membership fee if you are accepted, and then have to wait at least 48 hours before being admitted. On the other hand it is open to a member to sign in a guest at any time although remaining responsible for the conduct of the guest. Casinos, of their own accord, usually set a minimum standard of tidiness in dress which they require their members to observe. This doesn't mean that ladies are expected to wear their diamond tiaras, but they could well be turned away for being clad in those inelegant jeans.

The full details are not immediately relevant, but the Gaming Act prohibits the serving of alcoholic drink at the tables, (befuddled punters could throw their money away even more recklessly than usual, or exhibit one or more of the familiar aspects of drunkenness), enforces strict rules regarding money; credit is prohibited, and cheques must be very promptly presented to a bank; and prohibits gratuities to such of the staff as dealers, supervisors or managers. Waiting, and bar-staff are excluded, and appear to do very well in a climate where the value of money seems to be the punters' last consideration. The Act also imposes certain protective rules for Blackjack.

Forget any idea of crooked play. You should soon enough learn that casinos have no need to cheat. Cardsharps and "fixed" wheels are for the film industry -- and just possibly for a few remote locations in the world. This doesn't relieve you of the need to check that you receive the correct number of chips when buying them or when being paid for winning bets, or that you are paid the right amount when cashing in your chips -- in the literal sense! Unintentional human errors are possible, and a dealer may occasionally lapse as a result of changing from a table with coloured chips of a higher or lower minimum value. In the main, dealers seem to be surprisingly efficient in view of the many and complicated pay-outs they may be called on to make. Supervisors should approve every transfer but they can very occasionally show a degree of boredom and inattentiveness.

Roulette was a brilliant invention. The wheel comprises 37 slots, 36 coloured alternately red and black, and one, for Zero, being neutral. 34 of the adjoining numbers are alternately odd and even but the numbers are not in numerical order. This is a representation of the wheel:-

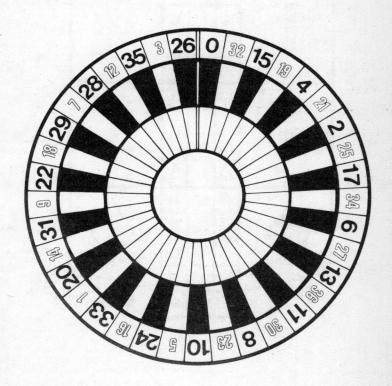

As you see, with the exception of numbers 5 and 10 which are next to each other, the numbers alternate between high (19 to 36) and low (1 to 18). As far as possible, all the even chances are spaced equally round the circumference of the wheel, and whenever that was not possible, the adjustments balance one another. For example, six pairs of odd are adjoining (25/17, 27/13 etc.), and they are balanced by six pairs of adjoining evens (30/8, 16/24 etc.), although 26 and 32 are separated by Zero. They, incidentally, are the only two high numbers which would have adjoined each other. It was all worked out in a beautifully symmetrical way.

Bets may be made in a variety of ways but must be placed on

the layout before the croupier finally calls, "No more bets". This is the layout of the table on which bets are placed:-

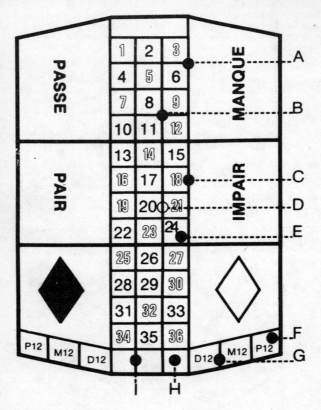

- A. Transversale — 6 numbers.
- B. Carre — 4 numbers.
- C. Transversale — 3 numbers.
- D. Cheval — 2 numbers.
- E. Number, *en plein* — 1 number.
- F. Dozen — 12 numbers.
- G. Two dozens — 24 numbers.
- H. Column — 12 numbers.
- I. Two columns — 24 numbers.

These, together with their winning odds, are the possible bets which may be covered by a single chip:-

1. 1 number: sometimes called "straight up" (including 0), 35/1
2. 2 Nos: placed on the line dividing them ("cheval") 17/1
3. 3 Nos: placed on the edge of a line such as 10-11-12 ("transversale") 11/1
4. 4 Nos: placed in the middle to overlap all four (carre'") 8/1
5. 4 Nos: the first four, i.e. 0-1-2-3 8/1
6. 6 Nos: as with three numbers but covering two rows across the layout: 5/1
7. 12 Nos: a total column either (1-34, 2-35 or 3-36): 2/1
8. 12 Nos: a complete dozen, (1-12, 13-24 or 25-36): 2/1
9. 18 Nos: of red/black, odd/even or high (19-36) or low (1-18): 1/1

None of the quotations from 35/1 down to 2/1 has any mathematical advantage over another. Ignoring Zero for the moment, your true chance of finding the winning number from 36 is 35/1. If you backed two 35/1 chances, one of which must lose, your return of 34 from the other (35 winnings less one loss), represents 17/1 to your outlay -- exactly what the casino pays for one chip on two split numbers. If you backed six separate numbers, five of which must lose, your winning return is 35 minus five equals 30, and 30 to six stakes is the simple 5/1. The arithmetic is impeccable.

There is a slight difference with the even-money chances in that when Zero claims the stakes on the numbers other than Zero itself, the even-money backers lose only half their stakes. As already hinted, you will be shown how to cope with the the "impossibility" of winning on even chances.

To avoid endless arguments and prevent cheating between players, each table has its own supply of differently coloured chips with an emblem exclusive to that table, and they will be valued at the minimum amount acceptable as a bet unless the player, at the time of purchase, asks for a higher value and pays accordingly. It means that when the dealer, i.e. the croupier, comes to pay, he can push the pile of winning red chips towards the person with the red chips in front of him, and so on. A supervisor or "pit-boss" is stationed so that he can counter-check whatever payments the dealer may be intending to make, to adjudicate about matters arising during the play, and generally to control the game.

There are also cash chips of various denominations between, say, 50p and £100 -- and sometimes much larger. As cash chips are identical it does leave it open to two people to claim a winning bet as theirs. All gaming is now continuously recorded by video cameras so most disputes can be settled by that means, however, arguments are a nuisance besides holding up the game.

The reward for backing a winning number at Roulette is 35 times your stake, which you also retain. Every other bet is in exact proportion to that 35/1. Of all the casino games Roulette most obviously relates to arithmetic, and this is the point at which it must be strongly stressed that the arithmetic we are dealing with is that of the extremely long term. It is mathematics based on performance over an idefinitely long period of time; in a word, of infinity.

For our purpose, the most comparable example is the tossing of a coin. It is generally understood that the eventual result of spinning a coin is an equal number of heads and tails. On the way to that parity, although there will be runs where heads and tails alternate in a way you might look at as the most likely, there will also be groups of all heads or all tails as well as runs in which no pattern predominates. You should clearly understand that no sequence of results can fall anywhere except into one of those three categories.

Also in this context, there is no way of identifying or defining normality. If you see 20 consecutive heads, it isn't to be thought of as abnormal, because all you are witnessing is a factual trend or cycle which is attributable to <u>short-term</u> arithmetic and is, in the present fraction of time, defying infinity. Stated in its simplest terms, this reliance on short-term arithmetic is what you are going to be brought back to time and again as the only way there is which gives any real hope of beating the casino. Even though our lengthiest session at a table represents less than a speck of time to infinity, the longer we play, the more chance we give that long-term arithmetic to operate against us.

At Roulette, every one of the 37 possibilities will at last appear an equal number of times, and in the course of that performance will produce an equal number of each of the even chances: reds, blacks, highs, lows, odds and evens, which, but for the interruption of Zero once in 37 spins, are identical with the heads and tails of a coin. It follows that the even chances at Roulette MUST fall into one of the three patterns similar to those of the spun coin. Give the player a means of identifying the type of a current pattern, and it is logical to suppose that he could make a profit. If you <u>knew</u> there would be fifteen consecutive reds, you could bet maximum on red for every spin and make a nice pile of money. Of course you don't know. Yet every run of fifteen reds starts with two reds, and every alternation of fifteen odds and evens starts with odd-even-odd or even-odd-even. All I have to do is to show you how simple it is to identify these runs, how you can turn them into profit, and afterwards how to organise yourself in such a way that you take away the greater part of such winnings.

Without prompting, you should now see that if you backed red for fifteen successful spins, ended by black, but continued to back red, your future expectation would be enough winning blacks to cancel your profit, even though your reds only balanced an earlier excess of blacks. This doesn't mean that in any case you could now rely on a run of fifteen blacks, although that could certainly happen -- amongst many other possibilities. What it does mean as an obvious conclusion is that the profit from a <u>short-term</u> trend must be protected from the ravages of the <u>long-term</u> counter attack. The requirement to achieve this is self-discipline. Without it, you fight a losing battle.

The numbers at Roulette present a more complicated pattern, but patterns there certainly are. For every number on the wheel to appear in 37 spins suggests the satisfaction of astronomical odds, yet nothing is impossible within the mathematical orbit. The commonplace, in which not all the numbers win in 37 spins, calls for some numbers to do so more than once, and possibly several times.

The wheel behaves in an entirely random fashion. People will quote, "The wheel has no memory." Well, of course it hasn't! It's made of wood and metal, with no brain even of the electronic type. The trap you must avoid falling into is the giving way to a mental attitude which believes that because a particular number hasn't won for some time it must win now, or soon, or that because one or more numbers have won several times each in recent spins, they are unlikely to win again for the time being. They can, and they will, often to the dismay of number chasers, win again, sometimes several more times in a comparatively few spins. At first it may be difficult to accept, but it is a vital fact of Roulette which needs to be assimilated so that not only does it fail to surprise you but is actually welcomed as something which may be looked for and used to your advantage.

If you chose to bet on No.29 for 37 spins and it failed, but No.28 won five times, you might curse your luck and ask how you could have benefited from that tantalising 28. It is usual for a few numbers to "sleep" for long, and occasionally very long times. A hundred spins? Yes, frequently. Three hundred spins? Yes, again, and why not?. Never allow yourself to believe that because 17 hasn't come up all the afternoon it <u>must</u> do so soon. Remember the pantomime chants, "Oh! yes it will," answered by, "Oh! no it won't."

AT ROULETTE THE ECCENTRIC MUST NOT BE REGARDED AS "UNBELIEVABLE". If you back one number for 18 spins its slot will have no better than an even chance of capturing the moving ball by the end of those spins because half the numbers on the wheel <u>cannot</u> win in that time. Not "may not", but cannot.

In the last century a perceptive engineer, later helped by other people, made lists of winning numbers at different wheels and, based on the theory that some wheels hadn't been accurately balanced, made a fortune by backing groups of numbers indicated by the suspected bias; proving, obviously enough, that his theory was correct. It took the casino quite a time to discover the secret of his success, but when it did, in typical fashion defended itself by changing the wheels from table to table. The next time the engineer and his friends returned to back their indicated numbers, they were the ones most likely to be appearing at different tables. We might suppose that with modern technology an unbalanced wheel is unlikely, although because of the nature of patterns and trends, you may be led to think so when a certain quarter of the wheel dominates the results for a time. Yes, and moving parts do wear with use.

Presently, we'll examine the theory of "neighbours", a popular and sometimes acceptable standardised wager on a number and the adjoining two on either side of it. We will also consider the myth that a dealer is able to spin the ball so as to bring up any number at will.

Because, as illustrated, every price offered for every available bet is an exact proportion of 35/1 the true challenge must be understood and faced. Should you decide that as 27 is your particularly lucky number, (you are an "astrologist" and not a mathematician!), you will back it for one chip a time and ignore everything else. Say you do this for 111 spins. Giving every number including Zero its proper share of the action, your "expectation" should be three wins: 111 divided by 37. You expect more than three wins because you are going to be "lucky". If the mathematical expectation is realised, you will receive three times 35, which is 105 chips and you will save three winning stakes. So your return from 111 spins is 108 chips and the casino has pocketed three of your stakes: its 2.7% stated advantage.

If you had backed two numbers throughout and each won three times, the casino would have won three chips for each series; and so on. Thus if you backed ten numbers every time at £1 each for a total outlay of £1,110 your expected wins would return £1,080 and cost you £30. That 2.7% isn't the only fly in the ointment. If your 27 didn't come up three times, you could lose £39 if it won only twice, £75 if it won only once, and £111 if it slept throughout. In that event you would lose 100% of the capital involved. Nor would it matter whether there were eight Zeros or no Zeros. Any of the remaining numbers rob you of your stake if your own number fails to oblige. Dodgy, isn't it?

The reversed situation is when your number wins on the first spin. The ball, running counter to the direction of the wheel, bobs against the metal obstructions, hits a slot but is travelling too fast to be caught yet, scurries across more slots, is settling in No.6 but just trickles over the edge into No.27. "Twenty-seven, red, odd," announces the dealer as he places the plastic "dolly" firmly on your beautiful chip. What's that? A three-thousand-five-hundred percent gain? Who's talking about 2.7%? You'll take your money and go? Unthinkable, isn't it? You'll explain that you came for some fun. It's a bit hard that anyone should expect you to call it a day after a single, solitary spin. Besides, you felt in your bones that the lovely No.27 was going to be kind to you. Why shouldn't it win again?

Now you've got a nice lot of extra money, why not try with two chips on No.27? After all, you can't win if you don't play, and don't people urge you to press your luck? Fair enough, but whether or not you double your stake, it is much more important to decide if you are going to sit there while your 35-chip win disappears and is followed by more, perhaps a lot more, of your original chips. If you go primarily for entertainment and are willing to pay the price, that is your choice. If your aim is to win money, you will need to cultivate a more miserly outlook. Of course your 27 could win again at once or quite soon, and induce mild euphoria. Good for you. You will read nothing here which would condemn you for taking the fullest advantage of how the wheel is currently behaving. This theme is further expanded in the investigation into "Hot numbers". The only warning word is not to let euphoria overwhelm prudence.

I had been playing for about an hour when a man came to the table, changed £500 for £5 chips and put ten of them on No.32. He went on to put ten each between 32 and 35, (a split, or cheval), between 32 and 31, between 32 and 29 and between 32 and 33. As you may have supposed, the only reason for describing the bet is because 32 won. The payout was for £50 at 35/1 and four times £50 at 17/1 for the four split numbers. A cool, if you'll pardon the expression, £5,250 for one bet without losing another chip anywhere else on the table. "Thank you," he said to the dealer. "Not a bad afternoon's work. I think I'll cash in," and he took his money and went.

Except for his comment, I should have doubted that it was his only bet of the afternoon. He could have been winning or losing at other tables. If he normally bet £250 a spin he wouldn't have been stunned by a win of that size. It's all a matter of proportion. One player's £1 is another man's £100, and big stakes account for big losses as well as eye-catching wins. This illustration wasn't an intentional praising of someone who won and quickly retreated with the loot, although there might have been reasons why it was a good decision. Only he knew why he chose No.32. You can often see which are the "favourite-number" players. One man backs the date, month and year of his birth, often running between two tables for twin attempts. Like any other hit or miss method, it gives him wonderful days as well as desperately bad ones.

The trouble with Roulette is that there is nothing to tell you whether you should stay on for more profit, or take to your heels with your winnings. As you see, by coincidence or otherwise it is possible to go to a table, put on your bet, and be right first time.

If you do have a decent win in relation to your personal capital and then cry yourself to sleep because you subsequently lost it all and more besides, who can you blame? For a start, yourself for being such a carelessly optimistic mug.

I offered to look gambling in the eye for your benefit. Apart from the mathematical odds guaranteed to any casino, it has some more extremely tough allies. Top of the list must be greed. Greed urges you to try to win more after you have won some -- and then to go for more and more. It tends to trap you into thinking that because you've won it's reasonably easy to win. Easy, it ain't, and you'll probably begin to ignore the odds. Greed encourages you to believe that now you have a pile of their money it costs nothing to increase your stakes and perhaps back more numbers as well. In that way, people argue, you have more chance of catching the winning number.

Greed fails to teach you that backing many numbers makes it much more likely that you will find the winner, yet that doesn't necessarily result in winning money. It can mean a few losing spins before the winner is caught, by which time you have laid out more stakes than the value of that eventual win. What is so special about "their" money? If you are realistic, after you have won it, it is <u>your</u> money. Why should you suddenly alter your plan of campaign? Certainly increase your stakes in proportion to your increased capital, but don't allow greed to displace prudence. As a gambler you are essentially a risk-taker but it is possible to be a circumspect risk-taker. If you are a compulsive gambler you are probably aware that you'll never beat the casino. You cannot be bothered with common sense, are never satisfied with your wins, cannot stop yourself giving back what you have won, and usually keep increasing your stakes in the forlorn hope of regaining ever-increasing losses. Alternatively, you won't allow yourself to believe that such things apply to you. If you are genuinely striving to be a clever gambler, watch out for greed.

Two other casinos' allies are the depth of their financial pockets and the unlimited time they have. Mostly they are open from 2pm until 4am every day of the year except Christmas Day, (in America it is a 24-hour daily opening), with their staff working in shifts. A 14-hour session should exhaust the most avid gambler, money-supply aside. Ranged against infinity, a few hours are invisible, but undoubtedly the longer you play against the odds the more likely they are to defeat you.

IT HAS TO BE SAID THAT THE **MATHEMATICIANS OFFER NO SHRED OF HOPE THAT A PUNTER CAN OVERCOME ADVERSE ODDS BY A MANIPULATION OF STAKES**. This warning is contrary to the long-held beliefs of gamblers, many of whom have, and do, spend many hours trying to devise staking sequences to combat the losing runs in their favoured game or sport. Staking is certainly important enough to demand a chapter of its own.

The last ally on the casinos' list is psychology. They set out to be cosy, intimate and welcoming, with music mostly in the background rather than the foreground, and not a clock in sight to remind you how long you've been playing or perhaps that you'll be late home for dinner. The staff are uniformly well dressed and well drilled in "yes, sir," or "no, madam." Complimentary food and drink, (non-alcoholic, thanks to the Gaming Act), can be had at the tables.

The average punter at Roulette smothers the table with random chips, singly and in piles, with frenetic industry. Occasionally a player is not satisfied with one outlay but rushes about between two tables, elbowing and dodging and quite likely making himself unpopular with his fellow gamblers. From this it follows that masses of chips are swept off the table before the payout takes place, but then someone has four or five stacks of 20 chips, together with some cash chips on top, pushed towards him. You just had £1 on your 27. "Fancy getting a big win like that! If I put on £3, at least I'd win £105." Do you see the temptation? You haven't taken into account the fact that the man who just won £400 was already £600 down, or that the lady next to you who picked up £68 from £4 on two split numbers had laid out £81 to win it. She didn't even count the risk.

To say that the odds are stacked in the casino's favour is no exaggeration. What do they care about a tiny 2.7%? They love paying out £2,000 on a spin and watching other punters splashing out in the hope of enlarged wins -- and anyway that £2,000 very rarely fails to be returned either very soon or at a later date. Punters are inded trapped by their own weaknesses and these are exploited to the full by the ruthless operation of the gaming industry. So what about the good news? **THE GOOD NEWS WILL COME.**

Apart from the clever engineer, people have continually tried to devise a system for winning at Roulette. A man I met many years ago told me that after the 1914-18 war he and three other demobilised soldiers went on holiday to a casino-town in France and stuck steadfastly to the even-money chances. If red showed, they followed it until it lost. Then they switched to black. They had the luck they deserved after that awful war and their terribly risky staking-system didn't let them down. Their winnings paid for their holiday, and on their last night they had a balance which they lost on random numbers.

Their staking system is well worth examination because in similar form it has recently been recommended to me twice in a month, both times as a surefire way of winning on the even chances at Roulette. One informant did have the grace to say that it needed capital -- in other words considerable capital -- but I strongly suspect that neither was actually working the method. I first came across it within a year of my introduction to betting, and I'm sure it is quite familiar to many followeers of racing. I deal with it fully in Chapter 3, on staking.

CHAPTER 3

STAKING HIGHLIGHTED

It is quite impossible to live long in the world of betting before becoming aware of the supposedly vital matter of staking. This subject has always been discussed, written about, recommended, or decried as ineffectual, and at the risk of being hounded through the streets by those who want us to believe, (and apparently themselves believe), that male and female mental processes and instincts are precisely the same, I have to record the opinion that staking-methods are far more likely to appeal to men than to women. By the end of this particular investigation, that might look more like a compliment to the ladies than the reverse.

The obvious intention of a staking method is to maximise any gains from the chosen form of gambling, and it is often fashioned with the aim of recovering all lost stakes or at the worst, a good proportion of them. In the latter case, the balance of those losses is hoped to be won back as the staking continues; possibly from a fresh beginning. I will deal with a few of the well-known ways of staking especially where it is possible to quote from a written opinion, and in this way you may be able to judge their effectiveness or otherwise, and about their potential danger to your capital.

It is one thing for a journalist or article-writer to offer a series of figures in support of a favoured staking system, and quite another to know whether it stands up to the rigours of an arithmetical winter. With one exception, all the Roulette methods recommended in this book are based on the concept of level staking coupled with increases from enlarging capital.

First the doom-laden warning from a mathematician writing about Roulette, "There is no system which attempts to recover losses by mathematically juggling the size of stakes or which divides bets in the attempt to cancel the adverse odds, which is not bound to fail simply on account of those actual odds. No system is sufficiently safe and consistent to beat the game." To that, I want to add any form of racing, because those odds are stacked even higher against the punter. I think we may come to the conclusion that the systematic staker is blinding himself with optimism. He doesn't _want_ to know the mathematical truth.

I suppose the father of all staking systems is the infamous doubling of stakes after a loser. It shouldn't need a mathematician's pronouncement to explain that you cannot win by backing even-money chances on account of the inevitable losing run which will exhaust your finances. At Roulette, an additional hazard is the maximum permitted bet limited by the casino itself so that, for example, you could not wager more than £2,000 on red. You may already be shouting that such a sum is irrelevant because you're not going anywhere near £2,000. _Aren't_ you? Let's look at exactly what you would let yourself in for if you started to back a progression of that kind.

To win on even chances you have to double your stake every

time. Having lost £1 you need to bet £1 to win it back and bet another £1 to make the £1 profit. Now you have lost £3 so have to bet £3 plus £1 still to make your desired £1 profit. Your stakes have been 1-2-4, you are losing £7 and need £8 to recover and achieve the £1 profit. To make it starkly clear, follow the sequence 1-2-4-8-16-32-64-128-256-512-1024-2048... By the time you have suffered 11 successive losses, you are £2,047 out of pocket and need to bet <u>another</u> £2,048 just to make £1 profit. It is of course unthinkable. Make no mistake; despite the absence of any significant groups of similar results on my demonstration card, fifteen consecutive high numbers constitute no miracle, nor would fifteen consecutive alternations between red and black. If you had been backing low or the colour which last came up, your commitment would have been a disaster. Regrettably the mathematicians have the vote.

Optimists might argue that because even chances are involved, surely nobody would go far wrong by expecting to win most of the time by the fifth stake in any sequence. One hears so much about the "luck" in gaming. Was I "lucky" to have a method which was ideally suited to deal with those first ten numbers at that table? Was I "lucky" to have chosen to sit there instead of at the next table? Perhaps I was "unlucky" not to have arrived ten minutes earlier because there had been a red/black alternation of 20 spins which would have made £85 look very modest. Just the same, was I "unlucky" not to have chosen the other table to take part in a record-breaking run of black? Speculation of that sort is futile. All we can do is to react to what we actually see. Even if we missed a run of 20 reds, without knowing it, that random wheel is perfectly capable of serving up another run of 20 reds with only a single black to end the first sequence.

Yes, with good fortune or happy timing, you might get your wins up within five spins and temporarily keep out of trouble, but come the fifth stake you are 31 down, and then what? Arguing averages involves the inclusion of everything happening now, in the present, as well as what transpires in the long term. In this case, long-term is the extinction of your capital.

Before dealing with some other ways of staking, I want to illustrate two opposite opinions both of which appeared in print. <u>Doubling up</u>. Many years ago, in a booklet sold as a way to win at Roulette, came the suggestion that although the difference between heads and tails in 100 tosses would be a small margin, possibly not once would there be six successive heads or six successive tails. If you kept doubling your stakes, you would win only one point for each win, so you must create your own odds. The advice, therefore, in dealing with the even chances at Roulette was to assume that six successive losses would be rare, so you had to wait for three losses and then bet 2-6-14. This would win you either 2, 4 or 6 units. If you lost, the cost would be 22 units, but the encouragement was that the total wins would outweigh the rare losses. No comment yet, from me, about "rare".

The same man advised that the three dozens at 2/1 could be tackled by waiting for two losses and then staking up to six times at, (did you guess?), 1-2-4-8-16-32. These would give wins of 2, 3, 5, 9, 17 or 33 units which, he said, would store up a big margin of gains to balance the odd (?) loss. Too many losses at 63 units wouldn't be received with very great enthusiasm by me. The one safety-first provision was that if a series lost, it was necessary to wait for a win on that chance, and after that, for two losses before a fresh start. He did prove a profit of over 270 units from just over 100 spins, but then as the quick-witted lady said, "Well, he would, wouldn't he?" If you have a method to demonstrate, you want to show it when it is winning. Look at the first 12 spins in Appendix 1 for a start!

It happened that the mathematician gave the result of spinning a coin one hundred times. In his case there was a run of eight similar results, but he wouldn't have been surprised at double or triple that amount. He wasn't demonstrating Roulette spins but was relating coin-tossing to the even chances. On the mathematician's argument, the staking of 2-6-14 and the doubling from 1 to 32 would not in the end win you money. Prove him wrong, and I've passed on to you a very elderly winning system. But don't hurry away.

From a long time past I have been convinced that staking systems eventually become ironed out by averages. If, for instance, you regularly stake 1, 2, 3, 4 after losers, and in due course have 20 winners, would you agree that you were very likely to have five of those winners on the first stake of the series, five on the second stake, five on the third stake and five on the fourth stake? The very point of that sort of staking is the knowledge that you will have to put up with some losers between the winners you hope to find. If that is correct in principle, and you are backing even chances at units of £1, what will happen is that you will have five wins at £1, five at £2, five at £3 and five at £4, giving you total wins of £50.

The average of £1, £2, £3, and £4 is of course £2.50. So if instead of breaking the money into those different amounts, you simply bet £2.50 each time, you get your 20 winners wherever they fall, and again you win £50. I know this is all neat and tidy, but in principle I cannot see how you can effectively argue against it. What is so special about your luck that all 20 wins should fall on the fourth stake? The corollary to this is, unfortunately, that unless you can win on level stakes, you cannot win at all, a precept which by now is almost ancient history and is no exclusive discovery of mine.

Because I recoiled from the two methods described, and wanting to run a test of my own, I referred to the recorded spins of my latest casino-visit on 23rd March 1989, two days before this was being written. It was a particularly appropriate example because it showed a few of my methods in action, including a good win from the even chances. You can see a full description in Appendix 1. This is the list of my 113 spins:

27	21	20	3
29	34	28	36
34	25	13	2
1	32	35	27

10	17	2	1
5	3	24	4
11	16	32	29
6	11	13	26
15	29	31	1
16	8	26	27
17	26	12	16
16	7	8	0
22	4	6	1
7	9	3	34
6	17	9	30
11	10	34	15
11	24	17	11
23	29	27	15
36	11	15	13
25	16	21	30
7	31	33	3
14	26	23	31
7	29	24	10
0	19	12	27
5	28	5	36
21	11	13	4
28	3	3	35
36	17	25	25

==

Taking red/black and working through my numbers on the recommended staking of 2-6-14, I found 22 winning bets and 23 losing ones. Three times the full 22 units were lost. The overall gain was six units, made up from 72 net gains where a winner appeared within the three stakes, against the 66-units' loss where all three failed.

Odd/even was better. Now there were 29 wins against 17 losses, and a profit of 38 units made up of 82 against two full losses of 22 units each.

High/low produced the cloudburst. They ran up 34 losses against 18 wins. Seven times all three stakes were lost, reduced by four units because of two zeros. This time, losses of 150 and wins of 60, left a loss of 88 units, and a total deficit on the day of 44 units from the three even-chance groups.

The average from 2-6-14 is the unworkable level stake of 7.33, but if that were applied to the 143 bets I have shown above, the final loss would have been £36.65 instead of £44, and in this instance showed the futility of the stake-manipulation. Level staking, although still a loser, was cheaper. From the outset, I had no idea whether the man's system would extract a profit from those numbers, and I probably had a sneaking hope that it wouldn't, but firmly above that was the expectation that the staking would be shown to be no superior to an average level stake. In spite of my own opinion, I could hardly expect you to condemn a system on one set of bad figures. I do, though, ask you to look with the greatest suspicion on any planned escalation of stakes which have no relationship to increased capital resulting from winning. Having created a balance between stake and capital, why throw it out of proportion when capital grows?

As you will discover later, I do recommend a staking plan in connection with the even chances. Staking continues to rise for every successive win, and as there is no way of knowing the high point of such a winning run, there is no basis on which an average stake could be calculated -- that is, not until after the event.

Now let's turn to the system used by "the soldiers". You begin by writing down 1-2-3-4. Your first bet is one unit stake. If it wins, you cross off the one, and bet two units. If that bet wins, you cross off the two, and now bet three. If that wins, you cross it off and bet four units. If that wins, you start again with a fresh 1-2-3-4.

If your first bet loses, you add it to your numbers, and now have 1-2-3-4-1. You add the first and last together, making a new bet of two units. Should that win, you cross off the first and last ones and now bet 2 plus 4, equals six units. So after every losing bet you add the lost stake to the end of your string of numbers and for every winning bet, you cross off the first and last numbers which made up your stake, the objective being to be able to cross off all the numbers and allow you to go back to 1-2-3-4.

There is no question whatever that when things are going well for you, a most handsome amount of money can be made from this form of staking, and it might sound a little sour to hear that if things do go really well it doesn't matter all that much how you stake, because you'll win anyway. What gives me the shivers is the thought of what happens when things _aren't_ going well. As staking is such an important part of wagering I thought I must, for your benefit, apply this system to my own session on 14/3/89. Together with receipts and copy Income Tax Returns, I usually keep my cards for quite a period of time.

As off-hand you may not be familiar with which numbers are red and black, (those who are, may check them with my blessing), I decided to work on odds and evens as being immediately recognisable. So we write down our stakes: 1-2-3-4. I am not going to jump in with one of my own systems, but will use the one described by the old soldier, so that in every case I shall follow an even number by betting on even, and vice versa.

The first was 25, so one unit goes on odd. 8 wins. I write 1-2-3-4-1, and I bet two units on even. 12 wins, so I am plus 1. With the ones crossed off, I am left with 2-3-4 and a stake of 6 (2 plus 4), to go on even again. 33 wins, so I am minus 5, and write 2-3-4-6. 2 plus 6 makes 8 to go on to odd. 23 wins. I am plus 3, and am left with 3-4, making 7 to go on to odd again. 6 wins. I go to minus 4, and my stakes are 3-4-7. I lay out 10 on even but 9 wins. I am minus 14, and I write 3-4-7-10. Next stake is 13 on odd and 13 wins, so I am losing only one unit and am left with 4-7. 11 goes on to odd but 30 wins and drops me to minus 12. My stakes are now 4-7-12, calling for 16 on even. As 32 wins, I am now plus 4, and only 7 is left as the stake for the next even. 19 wins, I am 3 down but 14 on odd gives me an overall gain of 11 when No.11 obliges. So thankfully I can start again.

Tabulating the results may make it clearer.

Win No.	Bet.	Remaining betting-string	Win/(lose)
11		1-2-3-4	
8	O/1L	1-2-3-4-1	(1)
15	E/2L	1-2-3-4-1-2	(3)
34	O/3L	1-2-3-4-1-2-3	(6)
32	E/4Win	2-3-4-1-2	(2)
35	E/4L	2-3-4-1-2-4	(6)
32	O/6L	3-4-1-2-4-6	(12)
2	E/8W	3-4-1-2-4	(4)
33	E/7L	3-4-1-2-4-7	(11)
5	O/19W	4-1-2-4	(1)
3	O/8W	1-2	7
11	O/3W	--	10

Successful sequence, so begin again with 1-2-3-4

4	O/1L	1-2-3-4-1	(1)
29	E/2L	1-2-3-4-1-2	(3)
7	O/3W	2-3-4-1	–
31	O/3W	3-4	3
29	O/7W	--	10

Successful again, so new 1-2-3-4

2	O/1L	1-2-3-4-1	(1)
18	E/2W	2-3-4	1
17	E/6L	2-3-4-6	(5)
14	O/8L	2-3-4-6-8	(13)
17	E/10L	2-3-4-6-8-10	(23)
10	O/12L	2-3-4-6-8-10-12	(35)
8	E/14W	3-4-6-8-10	(21)
27	E/13L	3-4-6-8-10-13	(34)
30	O/16L	3-4-6-8-10-13-16	(50)
27	E/19L	3-4-6-8-10-13-16-19	(69)
20	O/22L	3-4-6-8-10-13-16-19-22	(91)
12	E/25W	4-6-8-10-13-16-19	(66)
33	E/25L	4-6-8-10-13-16-19-23	(89)
21	O/27W	6-8-10-13-16-19	(62)
20	O/25L	6-8-10-13-16-19-25	(87)
9	E/35L	6-8-10-13-16-19-25-31	(118)
28	O/37L	6-8-10-13-16-19-25-31-37	(155)
4	E/4W	8-10-13-16-19-25-31	(112)
14	E/39W	10-13-16-19-25	(73)
0	E/35L	10-13-16-19-25-18 (0=half loss)	(91)
23	E/28L	10-13-16-19-25-18-28	(119)
6	E/38L	10-13-16-19-25-18-28-38	(157)
25	E/48L	10-13-16-19-25-18-28-38-48	(205)
13	O/58W	13-16-19-25-18-28-38	(167)
34	O/51L	13-16-19-25-18-28-38-51	(218)
30	E/64W	16-19-25-18-28-38	(154)
21	E/54L	16-19-25-18-28-38-54	(208)
22	O/70L	16-19-25-18-28-38-54-70	(278)
27	E/86L	16-19-25-18-28-38-54-70-86	(364)

If you were betting, you'd have lost £364. Are you now going to lay out another £102 knowing that if it loses, the next stake in the series is £118? In terms of capital, you would then be committed to £584, that is assuming you were allowed to start at £1. I don't know anywhere where I can start for less than £2 on the even chances. In any case can you imagine yourself risking anything approaching £100 in circumstances where you were losing quite heavily from a starting bet of no more than £1? Most disproportionate, I should say.

Then I can imagine you've been thinking, "It couldn't be that bad. He's made up the figures just to prove his point." No, I didn't invent them, but if I had, would it make that staking method any saner or safer? Whether true figures or not, they show a fundamental weakness in staking in that particular way, and in our world of arithmetic there is <u>nothing</u> to prevent exactly that sort of thing from happening.

In the past I have used what I called "seesaw" staking when backing horses. This involved adding a stake for every loss, but deducting in round figures, the price of any winner backed. The effect is to keep one on the minimum stake if winners flow from the start, but with ten successive losers, 55 units have gone and the next stake is 11 units. This highlights the innocent observation that in order to win, winners are needed. Naturally, with even chances, the winning price is always even money. I haven't checked it, but shall we see if it would have been less disastrous over the last run? I cannot envisage a profit, but later on you will see how to deal with trouble. We start at 29 and back odd for one unit.

```
29
 2    O/1L         (1)
18    E/2W          1      (Winning, so revert to one unit)  W    1
17    E/1L         (1)                                                -
14    O/2L         (2)                                            L  (2)
17    E/3L         (3)                                               (5)
10    O/4L         (4)                                               (9)
 8    E/5W          5      (Reduce by one)                           (4)
27    E/4L         (4)                                               (8)
30    O/5L         (5)                                              (13)
27    E/6L         (6)                                              (19)
20    O/7L         (7)                                              (26)
12    E/8W          8      (Reduce by one)                          (18)
33    E/7L         (7)                                              (25)
21    O/8W          8                                               (17)
20    O/7L         (7)                                              (24)
 9    E8/L         (8)                                              (32)
28    O/9L         (9)                                              (41)
 4    E/10W        10                                               (31)
14    E/9W          9                                               (22)
 0    E/8L   half (4)                                               (26)
23    E/9L         (9)                                              (35)
 6    O/10L       (10)                                              (45)
25    E/11L       (11)                                              (56)
13    O/12W        12                                               (44)
34    O/11L       (11)                                              (55)
30    E/12W        12                                               (43)
21    E/11L       (11)                                              (54)
22    O/12L       (12)                                              (66)
27    E/13L       (13)                                              (79)
```

You understand that this was a demonstration of the use of a known staking system but not a recommendation that its application could win you money regardless of the chosen source of expected winners. Between the two methods, this one is far less costly, and yet on the results to be dealt with, to go into profit it would have needed eight wins in a row, or, for example, 23 spins in which wins were in the ratio of 3 to 2.

The earlier method with its potentially very high stakes would, at the point reached, have put you in profit with four consecutive odds or evens. Counting on through my cards, (incidentally the next three bets would have been losers), for 58 more spins, there were four groups of three odds (yielding two bets each), three groups of three evens, one with zero spoiling it, and, right towards the end, one group of four evens.

If all systems requiring rising stakes after losers are to be tarred with the same brush; and the mathematicians say they are; there is no particular advantage in dealing with a number of them in great detail, but it may be worth referring to a few of the more obviously popular ones, thus:-

(a) Progressions which might be based on chosen odds; betting at 6/4 against known 2/1 chances, or betting at 5/1 against, say, the 12/1 dozens at Roulette.

(b) Betting to win a fixed amount and recover current losses. This depends on the odds one is opposing, and about which my own warning has been forcibly expressed.

(c) Always betting a percentage of one's running capital. This is often recommended as 10%. The idea is that before making each bet you look at your capital and wager a tenth of it. The result is that you continually increase your stakes when winning, and reduce them in face of losing runs. Of course this method cannot be adopted for Roulette because you cannot bet £1.90 after a £1 loss from £10, and so on. I read that it doesn't "work" but cannot remember the argument against it.

(d) The well-known system used by the soldiers. When good; marvellous. When bad; desperate. I don't have a title for it.

(e) The "seesaw" idea in which there is a one-point increase after every loser but the reduction by the value of every winner.

(f) What my old racing-friend and I used to call the "team" method. This meant breaking long losing runs into halves and thirds and quarters; condemned by the mathematician.

(g) Any other systems you can think of, from complicated multiple-bets to the waiting for a specified number of losses before applying a staking progression. Doubles, trebles and suchlike are popular. I once read that any series of selections which win on level stakes will win more when backed in doubles, BUT no losing series of level-stake selections will win in doubles. Groups of three selections speak for themselves because you need two right for a winning double. Groups of four, involving six doubles, could have two right at even-money and two wrong; an all-square situation; but your return from doubles would be four units against a loss of five units. With five selections, (10 doubles), and only two correct at even money, doubles lose you five units. For those two to make a profit of just half a point, you need prices in the order of 2/1 and 5/2, and, obviously, those would give a level-stake profit as well.

Despite the various dismissive comments about some cherished ways of staking, in fact you might do marvellously well with one of them for a few days. That it happens occasionally, is, I suspect, the main reason for the survival of otherwise flawed inventions. I suppose, too, that it would be a fair example of a short-term winning cycle. That would be happily welcomed except that all the methods seem to have a built-in provision for perpetual motion. That is, there is no braking-system to prevent your rushing headlong towards the long-term certainty of loss. Couple this with the punter's undiminished optimism, and no amount of battering will normally make him blame his system. If it looks as though I have knocked down too many walls, let's see what can be built from the ruins.

Record and examine a lengthy series of coin tossing. Eventually you will recognise the kind of basic behaviour met with in all aspects of both Roulette and Blackjack. The three elements march in trends, tendencies, cycles, call them what you will. Your even chances run as groups, occasionally quite large groups, of the one possibility or the other (red or black), so that in any case while red is appearing, black is absent. You will also meet short or long runs where red and black alternate in what you might think of as their natural function. The third and only other possibility is a higgledy-piggledy mixture which defeats your power of classification. In short, you couldn't predict the next result in the series beyond opting for "either or". This is no reason for you to give up in despair. Help is at hand. The cavalry is charging across the plain. Meanwhile, I recommend that you re-read this paragraph with extra care.

By now you must have been badgered into believing that arithmetic is king. It remains king but there is a pretender to the throne, and this is the arithmetic of the present or short-term rather than the regal arithmetic of infinity. Because, in the makeup of the balance demanded by infinity there are many imbalances, if we could identify these, couldn't we wrest a profit from them? If we could, often enough, and then scuttle away with a significant proportion of that profit before the King caught us in his counting-house, wouldn't that defy the people, mathematicians or otherwise, who claim there is no way of beating the odds? I'd hardly be likely to ask the question if I didn't think I had an adequate answer, so let's start with one of several ways of overcoming the "unbeatable".

CHAPTER 4

PROFITING EVEN FROM THE EVEN CHANCES

Having proved the impossibility of winning on even chances, here I am, suggesting that you can. The secret is to run with those sequences of similar results whether of the same element such as all reds, or alternations of two elements such as high-low-high. Two things you will NOT do. You will NOT double your stakes after losers, and you will NOT allow losses to run away with you. You have already had an example of the impossibly high peaks to which either a staking system or a stubborn nature could take you.

It is absolutely vital that you set a stop-loss at any table together with an early cut-out point for turning your back on losing runs. False optimism that a losing run "must" end is a killer. Your watchword must be survival. The firm recommendation is to fix your stop-loss in the ratio of £10 to £1 stakes. Try the Micawber philosophy. If you lose four times at £10 but win once at £50, you should be able to enjoy untroubled sleep. Roulette is a battle, and you know about, "He who fights and runs away..." Run to the next table. It may serve you better. If it doesn't, and you reach your ultimate loss for the day, RUN FOR HOME.

There will be days when those accommodating runs fail to materialise for you. There is absolutely no way of avoiding such times. What can and must be avoided is the crippling damage to your capital by the wanton chasing of success when the warnings are there, loud and clear, that it is one of the occasions when the wheel refuses to behave in the way you hoped it would. Eventually it will, but you certainly cannot afford to wait, losing money in the meantime, while with increasing frustration you watch trend after trend obstinately declining to continue. There are few instances where self-discipline is more profitable than in that sort of situation at the Roulette table.

The operation is quite simple. If you see two successive reds, two successive highs or an alternation of three such as odd-even-odd, (there must be three to allow you to recognise the fact that it is an alternation), you bet, individually, on the continuation of that state of affairs. So you back both red and high, and keep backing them until the one loses to black and the other to low. At the same time you back the odds/evens to continue alternating until you lose to the appearance of two successive odds or two evens. Those would give you a new indicator for following either odd or even.

Staking begins in the ratio of 1-2-4 and continues by the addition of one unit after each <u>success</u>. You will note at once that you may double your stakes twice, but this happens only after <u>winners</u> and not after losers. A losing bet immediately terminates the sequence on that particular pair of even chances. Once the third stake has won, no loss is possible on that series because you will have seven units in hand and will next bet five units. After that, either you will finish with a gain of two units or will have 12 units in hand and will bet six of them on the next spin. On a modest run of eight successes, two of which are "indicators" your bets are 1-2-4-5-6-7- (winning 25), 8-lose, net gain 17 units. If your first, second or third bets lose, you are down one unit only. You can immediately see how economical this is in terms of capital risk.

THERE ARE TWO NEVER-TO-BE-BROKEN RULES. Whether you are making one, two or three bets a spin, should you lose money on balance on each of three successive spins, you must stop. Don't place any more even-chance bets at that table. Secondly, should you reach your stop-loss, stop is the operative word. If you are following this system only, LEAVE THE TABLE. In any case further bets of any sort based on the system are _prohibited_ at the table. Remember, the fundamental operation is the snatching of short-term profit.

The second of those points will be self-evident. If you are playing at £2 units and you enter £20 in brackets in the outside column of your scorecard, (see below and the playing-example on page 38), that is your stop-loss ratio and there is nothing for it but to order yourself to stop. It _might_ be going to change for the better, but we cannot afford to spend money testing the water.

Applying the first rule, you must accept that regardless of the overall winning or losing situation, three losing spins in a row spell danger. For example an opening sequence of 1 (red) - 5 (red) - 19 (red) - 12 (red) - 4 (black) and 19 (red) would justify these bets:-

```
1
5
19      Red 2 Won:    Odd 2 Won:  Low 2 Lost:    Net plus 2
21      Red 4 Won:    Odd 4 Won:                    plus 10
12      Red 8 Won:    Odd 8 Lost: High 2 Lost:      plus 8
4       Red 10 Lost:                                minus 2
19                    Even 2 Lost: Low 2 Lost:      minus 6
```

You haven't reached your stop-loss of 20 but you have lost money to the casino from each of the last three spins, and that must be their last chance from that method at that table.

You are being offered a complete and successful strategy. Yes, by all means acquire your own Roulette wheel and practice and investigate to your heart's content. In fact if you do, make very sure that your test is a really extensive one. Against that, I beg you not to experiment with your own money at the casino. You may have yet to learn how cussed a cycle can be when it is running against a punter. It is for that very reason we "arrest" it the moment it begins to behave suspiciously.

Most casinos supply cards on which numbers may be recorded under their heading of red or black. You might find it best to list the numbers in one column on the extreme left of the card and use the middle of it for your bets, e.g. R1 O2 L1 and should No.5 win (red, odd, low), the next entries would be R2 O4 L2. Even if you are new to the game you will quickly learn which are red and black. All the other sorts speak for themselves.

For a different purpose, which you will understand later, it is helpful to enter in the second column the number of the relevant dozen, making your entries look like this:-

```
16-2
22-2
32-3
 1-1
12-1
```

When you come to classify No.25, you don't need to be told it is odd and high, (everything above 18 is high), and if you don't remember it as red you can check that from the wheel or, very likely, from the back of your scorecard. To enter your wins and losses, make a tick or an X on the right-hand side of the card, and in the very last right-hand column, show the running total of money won or lost. Losses can be shown in brackets. Remember, (10) says STOP if you are playing at £1. Never forget, either, that X X X in a row also orders you to stop. NEVER disobey.

The outcome of these rules is that you are likely to have quite a number of losing sessions. They will be comparatively small losses because you will be playing the game in that way. The credit side is that you must make the fullest use of the winning situations. This is no "stop-at-a-win" system. One thing you must never do is to allow yourself to believe that your luck is too good to be true. You have been cutting your losses to prevent them from becoming too bad to be true. Now you must on no account stop betting because you have had ten consecutive wins on low. Yes, obviously the run must eventually come to an end, but who are you to say that it won't go on for another five or ten spins? Or 20? Ten consecutive lows would be winning you £84 for £2. Five more lows followed by the losing high would earn you an extra £70. You need that £154. Don't turn your back on it.

One day you might sit in on a record sequence. Play it to the last glorious spin. It is unconfined joy to see £30 standing on red, (it cost you only £2), and not _really_ caring if it loses. By that time, for the original outlay of £2 on the red/black group, you would have won £28, £26, £24, £22, £20... and so on down the scale to the starting-point, and you would have watched only 15 spins, 13 of them carrying your bets.

The advantage gained by backing all three even chances as they qualify is that they can support one another while you are waiting for that successful run. The whole concept of the method is the cashing-in on winning trends. If your first two numbers were 2 and 6, you would have two black, two even and two low, and therefore would back all three to continue. At this moment you may be at the beginning of a good run -- ten black or nine low -- or at the end of a long run of odd -- you weren't there taking notes -- or at the start of a haywire performance by all the participants. What you do know is that unless the next number instead of being, black, even, low, is not red, odd, high, you will not lose all three of your stakes. For example, 28 is black, even, high; winning you two and losing one. 34 is red, even, high; winning you one but losing two, and 9 is red, odd, low; also winning one and losing two.

It doesn't mean that you can win only when you have to wait for an especially long sequence to occur. There will be times when shorter successes will tot up to an amount which stops you at a profit of £10 or more, either because three losses say so or because you are currently suffering more losses than gaining wins, so you decide to stop anyway. This is a very different situation from halting a splendid run simply because you "feel" it can't go on any longer. Our business is to follow fact. Guesswork at gambling gets you nowhere in the end.

Zero will claim half the money wagered on the even chances and to that extent obviously inflicts a loss. It does not, however, prevent your sequences continuing as before, because in any event, being neutral, it cannot give indications for future play; with the one exception that three Zeros in a row would be three consecutive losses and therefore an order to stop. Probably the best way to cope with Zero is to leave your stakes on the table after the dealer has removed the forfeited half, and then play as though Zero had not intervened. Mark your X for the losing spin. If your stake was the minimum allowed at that table or if, after half has been removed, the remainder is below the stated minimum, you will have to make the necessary adjustments if the rules have not ordered you to stop. That Zero might have caused a third X and given you your marching orders.

The alternative way of dealing with Zero is to accept the loss, remove the remaining chips and then re-stake the existing sequences from the beginning. This does have its merits when Zero shows signs of becoming hot, but needless to say that is evident only when it has started to happen. Zero, like any other number on the wheel, has its purple patches and as you will discover in Chapter 8 such phenomena can be turned to profit on many a happy occasion.

An advantage gained by making complete entries as you bet is that you can later analyse your performance for possible oversights or errors of judgment, and in this instance allows me to give you an action replay of a successful session from the fairly recent past. It should help you to a quicker understanding of the method. Incidentally, when following alternations, I make a heavy dot against the stake as a reminder to keep changing the bet for as long as that alternation continues. This is how I dealt with the first seventeen numbers, at that time played at £1:-

```
8     (on the wheel when I sat down)
0
2
1     B1x    E1x    L1W    x    (1)    (losing one stake)
10                  L2W    /     1     (net plus one stake)
31    R1*x   O1*W   L4x    x    (3)    (two alternations *)
29    B1W    E2*x          x    (4)
2     B2W    O1x    H1x    -    (4)
4     B4W                  /     -
26    B5W    E1W    L1x    /     5
```

```
33    B6W    E2x              /    9
35    B7W           H1W       /   17
19    B8x    O1W    H2W       x   12
35           O2W    H4W       /   18
 7    R1*W   O4W    H5x       -   18
17    B2*W   O5W              /   25
 5    R4*W   O6W    L1W       /   36   (net win so far)
      ===============================
```

The casino has now been beaten. Although the next spin calls for an outlay of 14 chips, (5, 7 and 2), you would forfeit your good conduct badge if you allowed too much more of that 36 winning total to escape from your grasp. Short-term arithmetic is showing its paces. You must keep with it until it outruns you, but then drop out of the race. The sequence of numbers continued in this way:-

17 (Black), 1 (Red), 35 (B), 13 (B), 11 (B), 25 (R), 33 (B), 5 (R), 35 (B), 8 (B), 25 (R), 16 (R), 15 (B), 22 (B), 27 (R), 8 (B), 35 (B), 8 (B), 20 (B), 18 (R), 5 (R), 10 (B), 27 (R), 35 (B), 14 (R), 12 (R), 25 (R), 25 (R), 21 (R), 6 (B).

Now for some homework. Test yourself by continuing the staking on the series. Write down the net winning total, (you see, whatever the result I'm relying on you to take money away from that table), and only after that, return here to see whether your answer agrees with mine. No cheating, please. In any case you won't cheat me, and who would you want to impress anyway?

Answer. The betting has to stop after the 42nd number. You would have lost seven chips on No.15, won one and lost one on No.10, won one and lost two on No.27, and won one and lost two on No. 35. The net profit at that stage comes to 154, down from 163.

One staking-problem you are likely to encounter is when you are nearing your stop-loss limit and a fairly large stake is called for. Are you now going to stake beyond that limit? Playing at £5 you could be £40 down. Black and low have just lost. Odd has won on its second stake (£10), so now calls for £20. High calls for a first stake of £5. £25 would take you to £15 over your limit. If you stop now, it is just possible that you will see odd make a winning run. This is where I could sanction bending the rules ever so slightly. I would not make the bet on high, nor would I put the full stake on odd. Instead, I would bet £15 on odd, taking me to a £55 loss if it failed, but allowing me to stay in the game if another odd now won. In that event, I should be able to reinstate red/black and high/low as appropriate.

In passing, did you notice the behaviour of the numbers you were checking? In 47 spins No.35's slot trapped the ball no less than six times. That would have helped another method you'll be able to learn about, but it is something which happens to numbers all the time and is the sort of pattern which you will come to accept as nothing out of the ordinary. Other numbers scoring at least more than once include 5, 8, 13, 17,

27, and 33, which meant that some numbers were crowded out. This, then, is the basis of sleeping numbers. Some of the others are so busy turning up that a few are prevented from putting in an appearance. As you learn to concentrate on trends, so you will give thanks for those grouped numbers. None of that is relevant to the even-chance betting, (beyond the emphasis on the grouping of like results), except that if you were backing black, odd, high, you would welcome three No.35s in a row.

Numbers do of course repeat. Arithmetic says that for every 37 times No. 35 wins it will once be followed by another No.35, and for every 37 times *that* happens there will be a third No.35. Those odds, well in excess of 50,000/1, would not prevent your witnessing a treble during your first ten minutes at a table. Out of the blue, it could not be predicted but would represent the twin chances that first it happened, and secondly that you happened to be there at that instant in time. More of this in another chapter.

CHAPTER 5

FINDING FAVOURABLE FOURSOMES

One of the features of absentee or sleeping numbers is their tendency to compensate with extra appearances once they have again shown their faces. It doesn't always happen, and it doesn't have to occur at once, so we must beware of costly pursuit. Not only beware, but just don't do it! But if the books are to be balanced, something which has fallen below a recognisable average must sooner or later produce an above-average performance. Experience has shown that if you restrict your expectations and limit your outlay, there is a surprisingly large percentage profit to be made from some situations which are not at all difficult to identify.

Just as you can regard one number as <u>statistically</u> due to win in 37 spins, so you may surely claim that any four numbers should win in those 37 spins. I hope you immediately recoiled from the suspicion that after all the words devoted to self-discipline and not chasing numbers, I was going to allow you to nominate four numbers and start some wild goose chase. Good for you if you did! We are going to be more scientific than that.

Anyone who is familiar with the variety of permutation used in racing or football-pool betting will realise that any four from 37 amounts to a stupendous total of possibilities. It also means that in 37 spins quantities of those possibilities must become fact; some of them appearing several times. Our particular problem is to discover which they are.

The four numbers might be in a neat square such as is formed by 1-2-4-5 on the Roulette layout, or three in a line across the layout with the fourth anywhere in an adjoining line, e.g. 1-2-3-6, or they might be in columns: 1-4-7-10 or 20-23-26-29 or even 8-11-14-12 the 12 being in the adjoining column. Alternatively the four could be dotted anywhere on the layout. For our purposes, making identification and staking easier, it would be best to concentrate on close groups, those in a square or straight line being preferred. They can be backed for a minimum of two split chips, or four single chips, but give a better potential profit if tackled with an extra chip on the number which won and highlighted the previously absent four, <u>absence</u> being the key; that is, absence followed by presence.

As you have been fully primed on the forces ranged against you, there surely must be no mistaking the need for businesslike efficiency. Some casinos supply cards with the complete wheel and layout printed on the back. Others have only the wheel and various figures; perhaps numbers and the two neighbours either side. If your casino doesn't provide a printed layout you must prepare your own, preferably on handy-sized paper. You might even resort to a photo-copier. On your layout you can block out each number as it appears. Once in use, you will see how easy it is to spot missing groups of numbers. The one snag is that in a long session your chart can become confusing. Again jumping forward, you need to keep your chart up to date and to note the total number of spins at least until every number has been marked off. The reason for this is that you may want to make use of the last two sleepers as described in Chapter 7.

If your chart isn't clear, you may have to decide whether to start another one or to keep it and try to identify likely foursomes by counting back. When you are experienced, this may be possible although not infallible, and although there can often be quite a time between spins, occasionally you have very little time at all. It is as well not to become involved with more than you can confidently handle, the first essentials being that you don't bet too soon, (before qualification), or miss betting altogether. As we somewhat ruefully say to one another at the tables, "They don't pay out for the next hole." Nor do they pay out on what you <u>ought</u> to have backed but missed. A help in counting back is to draw lines at five-spin intervals on your chart or scorecard. I always do this before making a bet at any table. It is obviously easier to tot up in fives rather than laborious singles, and the greater the extent to which you can stay ahead of the game the better your chances of winning.

<u>THE METHOD</u>   Once a group of four numbers has missed for <u>not less</u> than 33 spins, watch for the moment when one of the four does win. This is the moment to start giving all four numbers three spins in which to win, staking one chip on <u>the</u> number and two more chips split between the four. If they fail for three spins you will have lost nine unit stakes, (whether 50p, £1, £5 or whatever you have chosen), and you stop. Forget them. Instead, keep a lookout for another four. If you do find a winner within your three spins, the return will be 17 chips to a single split, or 52 chips if the original winner occurs again. After that win, repeat the exercise for up to three more spins. As before, stop at three losses. Also stop at another win.

In view of the known habits of numbers to "sleep" but then often to return in force, it should not surprise you that the first qualifying number of a foursome should be backed more heavily than the other three. In practice you should find that an encouraging amount of profit is contributed by what I usually think of as the "marker" number which, as you may learn from Chapter 8, can readily mark the emergence of a hot (persistently recurring), number.

In the event that one of your numbers wins within the first two spins, you are assured of a profit. If the win is delayed until the third spin, at worst you will be all-square. Any win within the second three spins must result in final profit. Obviously, if the original number wins again in any spin in which you are interested, you will be sitting pretty.

I cannot repeat too often that you must not go on chasing numbers. Our entire strategy is based on short-term offensives. The fact that sometimes one of those four numbers doesn't win until the fourth spin must not be used as an argument to extend operations. The effectiveness of the method is based on a good percentage return on outlay, (and the size of that likely percentage might stagger you), therefore outlay must always be kept within strict limits. Should your four numbers have been missing for a great deal longer than 33 spins yet after qualifying, not yielded a win within the allotted three, there is a very slight argument in favour of waiting until one of the four again wins, (of course if that were 33 more spins there would be a fresh full qualification), and then making a limited attempt to regain your losses. In such circumstances I think I would lay out not more than two splits each time, and certainly not go beyond three losses. On balance, I prefer to stay strictly within the rules and accept whatever losses there are.

Never lose sight of the risk-element in Roulette. On no account over-stake in the hope of a big win. Watch miserably as the dealer sweeps away that increased pile of chips, and in the end you may find that you have too few when the next opportunity occurs. If that is the winning one, you'll probably go home a loser, heaping curses on yourself for your greed, impatience and even stupidity. We , not the casinos, make the mistakes!

Bearing in mind that beginners may quite sensibly prefer a cautious approach to Roulette, I have usually described the most economical way of playing the various methods, but because these foursomes do take time to mature, you may want to make something worthwhile from them when you have the chance. By all means bet as heavily as you can afford, but make sure that you have a protective cushion of capital. A reasonably safe proportion would be £200 to £1 stakes. Unquestionably the winners are there but you will be hard pressed to obtain a written guarantee as to "when". As I keep a record of all personal betting, I am able to report very satisfactory results indeed from this particular method. I strongly recommend that you keep accounts right from the outset. It is all too easy to remember your wins but forget the losses. Keep details so that losses are faced and profits allowed to increase your confidence.

Whenever your qualifying foursome falls within one of the three dozens; for example 15-18-21-24, the second dozen, or a square such as 1-2-4-5 in the first dozen; there is a potentially lucrative side-bet possible at 2/1 on the relevant dozen. You stake a level sum, (£5?), for the number of spins called for by the method. This entails three bets at most should the foursome fail to provide a winner, or up to three more bets if one of the four numbers does oblige. A useful feature of this method is the possibility that if the foursome fails to win in the given three spins there are still three chances that the dozen will allow one or more wins from the remaining eight numbers in that dozen; and of course it does happen. Similarly, with the numbers all in one column, you can bet on that column.

Although up to now I haven't tried this idea at the tables, I note that over a period of three months during which I bet 51 times when a foursome completely fitted in with a dozen, the result of backing the dozen as described yielded a net profit of 8 unit stakes. This profit was lifted to 36 units if instead of making single bets, three doubles were attempted, using the first three spins only in each case. It must be a matter of individual taste whether you back singly or in doubles. Singles certainly minimise the outlay because six was my longest losing run as against 18 lost units when doubling, but of course in gambling, guessing at maximum losing runs is a profitless occupation. My confidence in suggesting this method to you is the fact that I have made consistent profits from foursomes and therefore expect a reasonably frequent appearance by them. The downside, as they say on the Stock Exchange, is that with only one win in three you are left no worse off. Because of the expected "compensation" when numbers have been missing for a greater than average time, you may genuinely hope for better than one win in three. Given that, you are an assured level-stake winner. This should not allow you to fall into the mistake of attempting to guess which dozen (or column), will win next and habitually making single bets on it.

Without listing all the spins during which the foursome was missing, here are the closing stages from one of my own cards. My layout showed that after 40 spins no wins had been registered by Nos. 27, 30, 33, or 36, so I noted on the bottom of what was by now my second card, "27--36" as a reminder. The spins continued:

```
23   2   (the 2 indicating the second dozen. See Chapter 6)
14   2
19   2
12   1
21   2
5    1
24   2
19   2
4    1
28   3                                                          NET
27   3   Here it is and I circle 27-3 as the "marker".
7    1   Playing at £2 I stake  27/4, 30/2, 33/2, 36/2    Lost 10
1    1   Repeat bets. Nearly! 1 is next to 33.            Lost 20
27   3   YES, and maximum. Won £140 less £6               Won 114
15   2   Repeat bets  for up to three more spins. Lost:   Won 104
6    1   27/4, 30/2, 33/2, 36/2. Next to 27!     Lost:    Won 94
33   3      "     "     33/2 Won, 36/2. Won £70 less £8:  Won 150
```

The second win, (or third loss), ends that successful game. I clearly remember how the ball hit No.13, edged over to No.27 next door, and trickled into No.6, followed by my silent curses. I also remember the man who had been laying out £50 on the third dozen all the time those first and second dozens were rampant. He was driven out of business a spin before No.28 turned up. If you have time to watch, you quite often see people opposing dozens or columns or colours after two appearances. They are the players who haven't discovered that the winning way is by following, and not opposing, the wheel.

Although I was not betting on it, my recommendation to back the third dozen, (or column) when that foursome qualified, would have neither won nor lost because two wins at 2/1 were balanced by four single losses. IF the ball had stayed in 27 it would have given a one-unit profit on the dozen in addition to the extra profit from the "straight-up" bet. But, no, the casino doesn't pay out on "IF"... Notice, though, that third column bets made a net gain of 6 units from Nos. 27, 15, 6 and finally 33 after the two losing units on 7 and 1 had been subtracted.

CHAPTER 6

OCCUPATIONAL THERAPY AT 2/1

So far you have one system which may order you to stop betting after a few losing spins, and a system which entails waiting for a specific happening not less than 33 spins into the future. If, while you are waiting, you foolishly risk money on that No.27, it's quite likely you will throw away profit from your even chances or add to their losses, and possibly be unable to stake a winning foursome. So what can you do?

When, completely ignorant about Roulette, and going on holiday to where I knew there was a casino, I asked an experienced punter how I should lose least money at the game. He advised me to stick to the columns and dozens at 2/1. What I had to do was watch what the wheel was throwing up and keep with it, preferably backing two of the three possibilities with level stakes. If you are lucky," he said, "you can gradually pile up some quite decent wins. But if it goes sour, you'll waste your money trying to fight it. Some days the wheel settles down and keeps doing the same sort of thing. At other times it goes haywire."

On my first visit I sat at the end of a very crowded table with the columns right in front of me. From the detailed look we have had at arithmetical trends, you will quickly see that any two of the columns or any two of the dozens will together behave in one of the only three possible ways there are, viz.

(a) a run of two of them to the exclusion of the third; including a run of one of them against the other, e.g. the first dozen is excluded by the second and third, but currently all the wins are in the third dozen.

(b) a run of alternations constantly excluding the last winner, e.g. first column, second column, first column, third column, first column... or,

(c) a muddling mixture defying your attempts to predict which two will provide the winner between them.

It should be clear that the behaviour of the columns has nothing whatever to do with that of the dozens. Each will be playing out its own game, and while one of them might be dancing about crazily, the other could be leading you to uninterrupted profit. Sometimes both will be good; sometimes both bad.

My own solution, before I was aware that trends could be classified in the way I have just described, was to back the column containing the last winner and the next column to it in a clockwise direction. I reasoned that this would take care of a run of winners in any one column, so obeying my friend's advice to stay with the wheel. So if the first column won, I backed the first and second columns. As long as the first column won, I kept to the same two bets. If the second column won, I switched to the second and third columns. If the third column won, I backed the third and first columns.

I found that my idea worked very well right from the start. I had changed £10 for 50C chips (it was Malta), and although with many people playing so many chips the game was slow, I eventually realised that my £10 was now £20. Beginner's luck! But the beginner had chanced to hit on something which in part satisfied a more sophisticated mathematical approach, and this is not to diminish my friend's excellent advice. DON'T oppose what the wheel is doing. Gather the harvest <u>now</u>.

I cannot claim a constant level-stake profit for this way of betting, yet by restricting your losses when the wheel goes against you, this method is much less hazardous than the pursuit of No.27. A positive improvement which I now use profitably is based on sequences of four spins. With either the dozens or columns showing figures such as 2-3-2-2 you start at the fifth spin with one unit on each of the 2nd and 3rd dozens (23 in my shorthand), or the columns if they were indicated, and hope to see 2-3-2-3-3-3... while you continue to bet similarly until the end of the sequence, i.e. when the dealer takes your chips. Then you keep scanning the last four spins for a fresh sequence.

If your figures read something like 1-2-3-1 where every spin differs from the last one, you have an alternation, so now you start with 23 (dozens or columns), and continue by always omitting the previous winner:- 2-(back 13), 3-(back 12), 2-(back 13) and so on until that sequence ends.

A series of results such as, 1-1-3-2-1-1-2-1-3-1-1-2-3-3-1 which loses you money every time you think you have something to bet on, is dangerous and must be resolutely dropped as soon as it has shown its hand. Don't try to outlast it.

When doing battle at the table, you are very rarely going to find leisure time. In order to record bets which you can instantly read; and because if you don't note what is happening you are likely to be at sea when calculating gains and losses you need to adopt some sort of personal shorthand. Experience soon shows what best suits you. These are my standard entries:-

1/2	No.1 backed for 2 units.
1/2²	Nos. 1 and 2 backed as a split bet for 2 units.
12²	1st and 2nd dozens backed for 2 units each.
12/2	No.12 backed for 2 units.
13/2	No.13 backed for 2 units.
13²	1st and 3rd dozens backed for two units each.
23/2	No.23 backed for 2 units.
23²	2nd and 3rd dozens backed for 2 units each.
1--3²	Nos.1, 2 and 3 backed as "transversale" (at 11/1 for 2 units
1--6²	Nos.1, 2, 3, 4, 5 and 6 backed as "sixainne" (at 5/1) for 2 units
1--5²	Nos.1, 2, 4 and 5 backed as "carré" (at 8/1) for 2 units
0/2	Zero backed for 2 units.
0/2²	Zero and 2, split for 2 units (of course at 17/1)
0²	Odd numbers backed for 2 units (at 1/1).
R2	Red numbers backed for 2 units (at 1/1).
H2	High numbers (19 to 36) backed for 2 units (at 1/1)

and similarly for Even, Black and Low.

st42   Applies to Zero, 1, 2 and 3: two units at 8/1.
Represents the heavy dot I put against the stake to remind me to change bets when backing alternations. For example, after red, black, red, my bets might go R1*, B2*, R4*, B5* and so on. Or if the dozens read 2, 3, 2, 1, I could be betting 232*, 132*, 122*, and 132*, depending how the sequence continued; although as explained below, I use ABC for the columns and not 1, 2, 3.

It follows that when I back a number, I put a diagonal line between it and the value of the bet, (1/10 means ten units on No.1 but 1--10² would indicate a foursome (1-4-7-10), backed at 2-unit stakes; this being shorter than the four separate bets shown in the example in the last Chapter), and when I split stakes between two numbers on the layout, as I have to separate them with a diagonal line, I write the stake towards the top of the number, e.g. 17/20². The difference between 13² and 13/2 is that the first one shows 2-unit bets on each of the first and third dozens, whereas the second one is a 2-unit bet on No.13. A dash (--) between two numbers will indicate that more than those two numbers are involved. It is used in the case of three, four, or six numbers.

One problem, the columns, remains to be solved. It is, simply, that if you write down 23², were you betting on two of the dozens or two of the columns? In fact, how can you see clearly for yourself which of the two options you should be taking? If you deliberately cut one of them out of your calculations you might well find yourself making a series of losing bets instead of the winning alternative. The satisfactory remedy can be achieved only by extra work.

The dozens are already officially nominated as first, second and third -- for our purposes, 1, 2 and 3. So the columns must be given different symbols, and insistently obvious is the alphabetical ABC or XYZ. Let's settle, then, for the first column (1 to 34) to be A, the second column (2 to 35) to be B, and the third column (3 to 36) to be C. That decided, it means entering the appropriate column-letter alongside the number of the dozen when each spin is entered on our chart. Naturally this will need to be rehearsed quite thoroughly if confusion and errors are to be avoided, for inaccurate information must lead to faulty decisions, and those, to lost cash. Charts will now begin to look like these three short examples:-

```
  7 1 A        6 1 C        33 3 C
 25 3 A        2 1 B        24 2 C
  8 1 B       28 3 A        23 2 B
 13 2 A       25 3 A        29 3 B
 20 2 B        3 1 C        26 3 B
 10 1 A        7 1 A        30 3 C
 22 2 A        3 1 C        14 2 B
 29 3 B        8 1 B        24 2 C
 29 3 B        5 1 B        21 2 C
  8 1 B       31 3 A        36 3 C
 18 2 C       36 3 C        32 3 B
```

Basing your decision on not less than the first four spins in each case, group one would have you happily backing columns A and B but ignoring the dozens because they failed to throw up either similar results or alternations. 1-3-1-2 was promising but the second 2 killed it. Then 1-2-2-1 promisingly started with 2 but immediately fell to 3.

The second group threw up continuing profits from the (13) dozens, but couldn't get its act together with the columns -- for similar reasons applying to the dozens in group one.

Group three showered you with profit because clearly both the dozens and the columns were in top form. This kind of trend does happen and can sometimes surprise you by its stamina. But before euphoria sets in, be warned that there is a fourth group. In this, <u>both</u> the dozens and the columns consistently refuse to cooperate, and, once again can display astonishing staying power. Your answer must be to withdraw from danger, at least by suspending betting on those dozens and columns, or else changing tables.

Once embarked on a particular sequence, don't vary the bets. The fact that the last four results are an alternation of 2 and 3 should not mean a switch to alternating bets, because that would bring in 1 in its turn whereas in this instance the cycle is telling you it is only interested in 2 and 3. On the other hand if an alternation you were following ended with 3-2-3-2-2, your 13 would then lose but 2-3-2-2 at once invites you to switch to 23 and stay with them until the next appearance of 1. A little practice should soon make it all clear to you.

You gain one unit stake for every winning bet; and lose two for a defeat. You are betting at odds of two-to-one-on, because of course you are covering 24 of the 37 possibilities. Zero beats you but as it is neither a column nor a dozen, you repeat your bet. There is one safety-play. It applies only to the dozens and not unless you are playing either the first and second or the second and third dozens. It also needs four or a multiple of four unit stakes. If you were betting two units each on the first and second dozens, you could instead bet three units on low, (1 to 18), and one unit on 19 to 24. If low wins, you are paid three and lose one on 19 to 24, a gain of two. If 19 to 24 wins, you are paid five, lose the three on low, and again win two. That is no different from betting two each on the two dozens. The saving is when Zero appears. Now, instead of losing all four units, you lose the one on 19 to 24 but only half the stake on low. It works similarly at the other end of the table. Now three stakes go on high and one on 13 to 18.

The purpose of betting in the way recommended in this Chapter is primarily to keep you in the game and out of trouble until a bigger opportunity shows up. Your profit won't rise rapidly, yet can be quite good. As always, you must step back from a succession of losses.

I warned you that patience was an essential in the battle to beat the odds. There is something really rewarding in store. Study the next Chapter if you can cope with a patience-tester.

CHAPTER 7

SLEEPING PARTNERS

Returning to the theme of compensating wins after long or longer absences, there is a most rewarding way to profit for those with dedicated patience. If, as previously suggested, you mark off on your copy layout each number as it wins, you may eventually be left with two numbers only, missing throughout your vigil at the table. I use "may" because a few numbers might still be sleeping at the time you wanted to leave the casino. Sometimes all 37 numbers can be marked off in perhaps 70 spins. That is of no use to you. The minimum suggested requirement is for at least two numbers to remain outstanding at the end of one hundred spins.

Having seen your sleeping numbers reduced to two, and with one hundred or more spins recorded, (even if you had needed to go on waiting after the reduction to two), you are ready for action. Your patience will still be tested because you must now wait until one of those two numbers wins. Then is the time to go for a bumper win at a modest cost.

After such a long wait you are entitled to make it a reasonably heavy bet, though <u>never</u> out of proportion to your financial situation. Your maximum risk need never be more than 14 chips. The first action is to back both numbers for one unit each for up to seven spins. Should neither win, too bad, you risk no more. If one does win, double your stakes on each for up to seven more spins. If no winner obliges within that seven operation ends. If a second win is achieved, double the stakes again and try for a third win within a final seven more spins. Whatever happens now, win or lose, you must call it a day.

The return from three wins can be very high, especially if they are bunched together. To obtain a full dividend we need our wins in not more than 22 spins. Is that reaching for the moon? Hardly. Arithmetic suggests that in 132 spins two numbers should produce seven wins between them. You don't know when your two numbers previously won -- you weren't there taking notes -- but you do know there has been only one in the last 100 spins, or, if you had been made to wait that long, 150 spins. All you are hoping for is that this is one of the times when compensating wins occur sooner rather than later and with the numbers reasonably bunched together. As with all chances, you can expect to be there occasionally at the right time. When you are there at the right time, you can count on a profit worth waiting for; a profit eliminating many losing tries.

The greatest gain would be from three wins in a row. On the first one you are 34 units to the good. On the second, 68 units, raising you to 102, and on the third, 136, for a total profit of 238. Take heart, for one of those would pay for <u>seventeen</u> completely losing attempts. The lowest gain, resulting from every win appearing on the seventh spin of each series, would be 154 units. Even this would pay for 11 separate attempts. In that time you could confidently expect an average of three wins as a minimum; that is to say three occasions when all three sections of the scheme came up trumps.

Sometimes two of the sections will succeed for a limited profit, and at others one will yield a very small profit or reduced loss. For example, an immediate win gives 34 profit from which a maximum of 28 chips need to be reinvested. You shouldn't be too depressed at winning only six instead of losing the 14.

If you fancy going for a bigger win you could add one stake to the qualifying sleeper in the same way as in the foursomes method. To do this would mean adding seven units to your intended outlay or else waiting for a win and then adding extra chips from the return. Suppose your sleeping numbers were 16 and 25 and 16 won on the 110th spin, the best result would include betting 2-4-8 chips on 16 while laying 1-2-4 on 25, and for 16 to win again in the third series. It would be no surprise if 16 were to win twice out of the three sections and in those circumstances finance plenty of further sleeper-operations. There would be times though, the wheel being what it is, when it would be the 25 which won three times. Then you have to grin and take the rough with the smooth. Well, winning can't be so rough can it, even though rating as second prize?

Should your confidence need reinforcing before you lay out more on one of the numbers rather than the other, remember that you are dealing with sleepers. Sleepers tend to behave in two ways. One is to make other "comeback" appearances soon after waking from their sleep. Their other habit is <u>to go on sleeping</u>. In the present circumstances, the odds would seem to favour more wins from 16 than the reawakening of No.25.

I am always reluctant to offer as "proof", conclusions from dangerously short sampling lists. In this instance I can quote only what has happened when my money has represented my mouth. Dealing with two sleepers in each case, on the only 69 occasions when one of them won after an absence of 100 or more spins and was followed by one or more wins by either of them within the time-span described earlier, the qualifying number won 69 times against the other number's 36 wins. It was because of the building up of a significant lead that caused me to search for possible reason.

An alternative way is to treat your 14 chips as committed in any case, so that after each win you divide your total remaining chips equally to cover the next seven spins. How often it will be possible to do this with the correct round number of chips will depend on where the wins actually occur. What it is likely to do is increase the winnings quite noticeably. Although you do have to wait for your opportunity to carry out this scheme, it is no reason to chance your arm. Play it at an amount unsupported by reasonable capital and you are back with the mugs. Yes, it <u>could</u> come off, but if I know the wheel, you'll probably be taught a lesson. Believe me, I cannot guarantee that you won't have ten successive losses. The whole point of estimating the amount of capital required is for the very purpose of coping with losing runs. On the other side of the coin, with no more than ten failures, the eleventh try would have had to be a win, and a win could certainly dry your tears.

The action works out like this:-

You are playing at a table with a minimum £1 stake. Neither No.8 nor No.20 had won during the 120 spins during which you were sitting there but now No.8 has turned up, so at once you place one chip on 8 and one on 20. Ignoring, for the sake of clarity, any additional entries on the scorecard, you will write:-

8
    8/1   20/1   [1]   (to remind yourself of the seven-spin limit).
5 wins so you have lost £2   (2)

    8/1   20/1   [2]
1 wins (next to 20) but you lose.   (4)

    8/1   20/1   [3]
30 wins and you lose.   (6)

    8/1   20/1   [4]   +28
8 wins and your chips in hand are a balance of 7 from the original 14 plus 35 from this win: total 42. As you now have to cater for up to another 14 bets, instead of simply doubling them, you can raise them to £3: (42 divided by 14).

    8/3   20/3   [1]
25 wins and you lose.   +22

    8/3   20/3   [2]
20 wins, so you will regain 108 chips which raises your total in hand to 138, and your winnings to....   +124

Now you have up to seven more spins to bet on. You can either retain £12 of the original £14 and allow for staking at £9 each number, or you can put in another £2 and bet each at £10. On the basis of seven spins virtually to nothing, we'll choose to bet at £9, and assume that only on the seventh spin No.8 saves the day. By now 6x£18 (£108) lost leaves... +16

With £9x35-£9 (£306) to come, the operation ends with a grand profit of £322. Rather nail-biting towards the end, but surely well worth the trouble?

This is it without the intervening commentary:-

```
8
5     8/1x    20/1x              [1]                    (2)
1     8/1x    20/1x              [2]                    (4)
30    8/1x    20/1x              [3]                    (6)
8     8/1w    20/1x     win      [4]                    28
25    8/3x    20/3x              [1]                    22
20    8/3x    20/3W     win      [2]                    124
6     8/9x    20/9x              [1]                    106
      Less 5x2x£9 = £18 a spin   [2 to 6]               16
8     8/9W    20/9x     win      [7]                    322
```

End of game.

Clearly there is no especial magic about any two numbers. Two were chosen partly for simplicity and partly for economy. Anyone wanting to make more from the situtaion after watching so many spins, could use the last three outstanding numbers as two pairs. If 8, 12 and 20 were sleeping at the end of 100 spins and 12 at last won, there is no reason, finance apart, why 12-8 and 12-20 should not be paired and played as two separate sequences costing 14 chips each. If they failed and left 8-20, they could be kept as continuing sleepers and played when finally one of them won. The overall cost in that case would be 42 chips.

My own records cover about 125 attempts at the simple pairs, a few times at 50p but mostly at £1, and later at £2. These are some selected results as an illustration:-

12-30	12 won on	100th spin		xxxxxx12/ xxxxx12/ xxxxx30
25-33	33 won on	122nd spin		33/ x33/ xxxxxx25
25-27	27 " "	156th	"	x25/ xxxxx25/ xx25
14-30	14 " "	126th	"	xxxxx14/ x14/ x14
25-36	36 " "	126th	"	xxxxxxx and 42 spins before 36 won again.
26-32	26 " "	126th	"	xxxxxxx but next spin, 32/ xxxx26/ x 32
2-17	17 " "	150th	"	17/ 2/ xxxx17

These few in no way try to conceal the many abortive games, the near misses, or the frustrating times when as many as four out of seven spins threw up a number next to the desired one. In my case I believe that my successes have been noticeably lower than might have been expected. Even so, a clear profit of well over £1,000 is hardly cause for complaint.

I accept that this protracted kind of betting is not everyone's cup of tea, but then, you might ask yourself what exactly your cup of tea _is_ . It may have been chasing No. 27 and perhaps I have persuaded you to stop that sort of folly, adventurous though it may have been. For anyone with the necessary stamina, these sleepers can be a wonderful example of patience rewarded, and well rewarded at that. Also, while waiting you might find continuous opportunities for gain from some of the other methods described. In Appendix 2 you can see an excellent example of this type of session. The figures were in no way manufactured because that sequence of spins actually occurred in a casino and was recorded by a journalist.

In wishing you good fortune, the best I can offer is that you choose the favourable table at the right time. If none is worse than the example in Appendix 2 you will be able to do yourself proud. Time is a fact which has a habit of leaving luck far behind in the race for the winner's pedestal.

CHAPTER 8

THE PERSISTENT OR "HOT" NUMBERS

People often look more disappointed or dumfounded when a number wins several times in 20 or 30 spins than if their own choice fails to win in that time. It's as though they instinctively know they're fighting fate with their random numbers. The general belief seems to be that if a number hasn't come up, it "must" do so soon. If it has won, it has used up its quota for the time being. Should it win again quickly, that's rather surprising. To come up three times, leaves them thinking, and often asking, "It couldn't win again, could it?" Yes, it most certainly could; and not necessarily stop at that. I hope, (no, I'm sure), that by now you recognise the phenomenon as a normal example of short-term arithmetic's propensity for upsetting infinity's apple-cart. And suppose you didn't believe it? Then you'd have to accept it as the visible efforts of the long-term arithmetic to do its balancing-act. Take it whichever way you choose, there it is, happening.

This custom of events to take place in bunches is widely understood. You may read from an analysis of score-draws in relation to a coupon-number for the treble chance that some are "hot" and others "cold" numbers. The offer to you is to run with the numbers which have housed those draws several times recently, or to look amongst the "cold" numbers for those that "ought" to indicate a draw. If a match ends all square, it will appear against some coupon-number, but we won't delve into the mysteries of how, being No.15 on the coupon would influence the result of a match between a very weak and a very strong team.

The intermittent showing of hot numbers at Roulette persuades some players to seize on the situation and back those numbers for varying times depending on personal choice or conviction. They aren't bad judges. Time after time you are going to find that what the wheel _is_ providing is a far better bet than anything it hasn't _yet_ offered up. I met a man who refused to back any number until he had seen it win twice at least. When he did back the numbers qualifying in that way, he would usually keep increasing his stakes after they had won; not, I'm sure you realise, chasing after absent numbers with increasing stakes. In any case, his increases were not from spin to spin but between winner and winner. From my observation he did very well for himself betting in that way.

One man, apparently a rather cautious backer, used to wait until he saw a number win _three_ times within about 20 spins, and then back it for ten spins in the hope of just one more win. That was the extent of his involvement until the next hot number showed up. I'd like you to look carefully at some figures.

The trouble with figures is that if I relate my own experiences there's no way of convincing a sceptical reader that I didn't invent them in order to substantiate a dubious proposition. Nevertheless I'm lisiting 50 consecutive spins from thousands I can prove were spun at a London casino. You ought to study them before reading my later comments. Try to pick out what you think you could use, and what might surprise the untutored punter. The numbers are:-

3-25-4-25-6-11-16-25-12-2-34-31-13-13-7-8-21-15-22-32-12-10-32-1-5-3-26-28-6-22-21-22-28-24-20-18-22-24-22-25-32-20-21-34-22-30-2-9-22-9-14-32...

We could discuss this lot for hours. I turned over a printed page, saw those three 25s and decided that I could use them as an example. What an example it turned out to be! As I'd been stressing how, for our eventual delight, every so often there were bunches of winning numbers to be seen, let's award No.25 the title of "hot". I think I must make it clear that I haven't a set of rules with figures based on research to pass on regarding the play of hot numbers. I have backed them regularly over the years and with enough success to warrant describing for you how I have gone about it. Because of the compulsory wait of 33 spins before backing a foursome, I tend not to look on a number as hot unless it also has been missing for that sort of period before registering the first of its three wins. I am certain it is safer to include a waiting period rather than to jump straight in as I have suggested with this No.25. When you first come to a table, you have no means of knowing what happened five, ten or fifty spins before. The best advice is not to make any assumptions. Reserve your bets for qualifying situations which you have actually seen. Unavailable to you and a matter of hindsight to me, I have just counted back and discovered that No.25 had last won 52 spins earlier so was a very positive qualifier; and as you will see, despite its three compensating wins, was a loser in our terms.

The backer of No.25 as a hot number would have lost his ten stakes. He would then come across three 22s in thirteen spins, and would win on his fifth bet, putting him 21 units in pocket. If he thought 32 qualified for him in 21 spins, he could add 26 net units from his tenth and last bet, but 21 would be too short a qualifying period for me. Betting too soon becomes a kind of number-chasing, and this we realy must not do. The same argument restricts the bets to ten.

The man who bets after two wins would have had a quick return on No.25. His increased stakes would have lost 30 times before 25 won again, but that arrived just in time to contribute some extra profit. Clearly I should need to know the man's exact rules, (assuming he works to a predetermined plan) before I could give you details, but as both these ideas certainly have winning potential, I feel more than justified in drawing your attention to them and, as far as possible, indicating the advantages and likely drawbacks that I have seen. Of the two, my hot-number rules promise much greater safety. Or should I say, much less risk.

The clearest cause of loss to us is the wheel which behaves in too balanced a manner. We are particularly interested in "lopsided" results which allow a few numbers to push the rest into the background. A wheel continually turning up fresh numbers or which throws up a whole group of numbers which win twice but no more, cannot be counted our friend. There must be a limit to the total of twice-winning numbers we could handle, both from the point of view of space for recording bets on our card as well as the amount of outlay involved. Once again, it will need pre-planning to limit the quantity of numbers, losing bets, and capital risk. Clearly if you are tempted to try this sort of betting you shouldn't persevere with suspect wheels, yet when they're good they can be very, very good -- the one I have listed, for example. What a bonanza with 22 and its seven appearances. That started in time to pay for any losses on 13, 12, 15, 6, and 21. The last one, 21, paid its way with a win on the 14th spin. 32 chipped in with two wins after 17 spins. Six qualifiers look to be about the limit you could handle at any time, but I'd be very surprised if research into both these methods would ever be wasted effort.

Meanwhile, what about the lucky-number punters? A survey once showed that the three most favoured numbers were 17, 14 and 35. Oh! dear. 17 and 35 are so far sleeping. 14 managed to scrape in on the 49th spin, and that was only three ahead of 29, which is next favourite. You were warned not to chase No.27. That happened to be sleeping as well. I will count for you the ten sleeping numbers: 0, 1, 5, 17, 19, 23, 27, 33, 35 and 36. Just for the record, by the 96th spin (when 5 repeated on the 97th), the only one still sleeping was No.36, and it took another 110 spins before that one showed up. Also for the record, it then won again on the 23rd spin, 15 later, 16 after that, eight after that and four after that. A fine example of compensation: but you'd have gone broke chasing it earlier.

Although there were runs of eight even, five alternate red/black, six high, 12 high and eight odd/even, the even-chances method, after reaching plus 13, would have ordered you to stop, (losing just one chip), after three succesive losses at the 13th spin. I suspect that my American might have left winning two chips.

Even though you have been offered no rigid advice about these two methods; mainly because they have come to me more by observation than by direct word of mouth; I think their winning potential is clear. I also think that by the application of the general principles given and often stressed by repetition through the earlier parts of the book, you should be able to organise yourself a profit from either or both of them.

Unless you can improve them by your own researches, you could accept and operate these simple rules when dealing with hot numbers:-

1. You know that the number did not win during the previous 33 spins before its current win.

2. It has now won three times altogether within 20 spins.

3. Those three wins should be,
   (a) In a fairly close group, or
   (b) Fairly equally spaced within the 20 spins,

4. The second win should at _worst_ appear by the 12th spin

of the 20.

    5. You allow the number only ten chances to win for the fourth, (and last), time.

The sort of grouping which doesn't seem to be really successful is where two of the three wins occur either at the beginning or the end of the 20 specified spins. It's as though in the one case the number has run out of steam, and in the other that it was too much of an effort finally to produce those two wins. "Enough is enough" it seems to pant. It is when the wins appear to come more effortlessly that the momentum is most often maintained for the additional win.

Although you may happily notch up your win with the first chip ventured, my impression is that you are more likely to be successful after about the fifth spin and for that reason I have quite often laid out an additional chip for the later bets. With so many different statistics claiming to be recorded and examined, I am sorry to say that I have no figures to offer about this variation, but it is not expensive and I have had enough double-stake wins to encourage me to persevere with the habit when I spot one of these hot numbers.

CHAPTER 9

THE "SILLY" SYSTEM

The title is not intended to put you off, but the warning is that unless you are a dedicated "bookkeeper" as well as a not too busy person, this may not be for you. The basis is the putting of two sets of opposing principles into conflict, and because of that, there is a suspicion that it cannot be sustained on common sense grounds. On the other hand, it made nearly £1,000 to £1 stakes and then £2,320 in 73 sessions at £2 stakes, so who is to say it wouldn't make money for you? The mathematicians? But we're already defying some of their theories.

The labour is that it entails recording in one of 37 vertical columns, each successive winning number you have noted at your latest session. In other words you must enter in column one every number which wins the spin _after_ No.1 has won, and in column 2 the numbers winning after No.2's wins, and similarly for No.3, No.4 and so on.

You are now familiar with the principle of _eventual_ compensation after famine -- equilibrium must be restored to support the average state. You have also been strongly advised never to chase numbers because of their undoubted tendency to sleep. The question I asked myself was whether a way could be found to get in on the act when a number was compensating, without my falling into the trap of expensive chasing.

Originally, thinking about "neighbours" as a convenient grouping of three numbers, (popularly, neighbours cover five of them, two either side), I saw that if No.20 and No.33, the immediate neighbours of No.1, had not followed it and that No.1 had not followed No.1, on the last 37 occasions when it had won, those two numbers "owed" an appearance each, and so did No.1. If missing on 74 occasions, they all owed two appearances each. To which your knowledgeable reply is entitled to be, "And can very well go on owing for a long time!"

You would be absolutely right. Nor, as far as an individual wheel is concerned, can we know whether those numbers had done their duty just before we came to the table, or were going to do it immediately after we left. So, for the purposes of what I later named the "Silly System", we ignore every possibility beyond what happens in our presence. In addition, however many tables we visit, the spins are run into one continuous session.

Let me explain what I believe to be the logic supporting the original basis of my thinking. When anyone goes to a Roulette table, almost always quite at random, he or she is going to witness part of the long-term process which eventually constitutes the average performance of that wheel. It is impossible to gauge which numbers will sleep, (although on average some positively will); which numbers will beat the average, (although some surely will), by winning more often than once in 37 spins; and which numbers are going to comply with the average and so will win once in 37 spins. In my _short_ visit, the numbers behaving averagely don't interest me. The others do.

If I am going to be present at these sessions where some numbers will do better than average and some numbers do no worse than average, is there any reason why I should always be unlucky enough to have chosen numbers falling outside those two groups? Chance being what it is, the horrid answer has to include "yes". Against that, surely I can argue that averages being what they are, there must be times when things will go right for me. Does this look like the beginning of an argument in favour of backing favourite numbers? It isn't intended to be. That just isn't on. But I am putting forward the idea that some numbers can be selected in a way which could give them a superior chance to those chosen at random. To spotlight our numbers, we must first establish some records, and for that purpose a lined book of 37 or more lines would be best. In it, you rule up 37 quite narrow vertical columns which may need to spread across a double page.

At the head of the first column, you write a bold 1, and over it 20/33. They are of course the numbers either side of No.1. In the second column you write a bold 2, and 21/25 over it. To save you the trouble of research, these are the remaining headings:- 3 (26/35), 4 (19/21), 5 (10/24), 6 (27/34), 7 (28/29) 8 (23/30), 9 (22/31), 10 (5/23), 11 (30/36), 12 (28/35), 13 (27/36), 14 (20/31), 15 (19/32),16 (24/33), 17 (25/34), 18 (22/29), 19 (4/15), 20 (1/14), 21 (2/4), 22 (9/18), 23 (8/10), 24 (5/16), 25 (2/17), 26 (0/3), 27 (6/13), 28 (7/12), 29 (7/18), 30 (8/11), 31 (9/14), 32 (0/15), 33 (1/16), 34 (6/17), 35 (3/12) 36 (11/13), and 0 (26/32).

When you return from the casino with your card listing the winning numbers you have seen, you transfer them into your book. Suppose your first few numbers are 13, 16, 26, 2, 13 and 27. In column 13 you enter 16. In column 16 you enter 26. In column 26 you enter 2. In column 2 you enter 13, and in column 13 you enter 27 under the previously-entered 16, and, because 27 is a neighbour of 13, you draw a circle round 27. Should any number immediately repeat, you draw a line under it, so 1, 1, has the single entry in column 1, "1" . The point of circling and underlining is that you can quickly see what relevant numbers have or haven't appeared.

You already know there is no magic about neighbours. They are no more or less likely to win the next spin than numbers on the opposite side of the wheel. The reason for picking them was that they offered the simplest way of recording and identifying numbers which were either present, perhaps in quantity, or absent. You will quickly see that until you have accumulated a sufficient number of results there will be no possibility of making predictions from your columns of figures, although once in being, the process can continue indefinitely. An illustration is that until you have seen No.1 win 37 times you cannot judge how numbers 1, 20 and 33 are so far behaving in relation to the expected average -- whether below, equal to or above it.

When you had enough records entered, you would be able to research individual numbers if you wanted to. You might have noticed that No.5 hadn't won after zero for many spins, so you could check the zero column for confirmation, and then by dividing the total of the numbers in that column by 37, would find how many times No.5 would have won (after zero), if it had behaved according to average expectation. Are we on the "chasing" trail again? In all strictness, probably yes, but your bets on No.5 would be limited to the number of times zero won at each session. That could be nil, six, or whatever, but it is not the whole story; besides, you would not be chasing No.5 for a hundred successive spins one evening. The question I originally posed to myself was whether any of the numbers behaving averagely could be avoided, because if every one I backed won once in 37 spins, nothing would be changed -- including the casino's 2.7% "take". I suspect disagreement from the mathematicians, who would harp on about this immutable 36/1 chance; in which case the £3,000 profit was gained fortuitously and could be expected to vanish unless protected by the application of " stop-loss".

My columns were 43 lines long, and with every one filled, (some were well into the second page), I queried whether I could expect to see enough numbers as it were adjusting to the average while I spent variable times at random tables, to allow profitable betting. I decided it was possible because surely not all the numbers could fool me all the time. Making due allowance for the eccentric bunching of winners and the expected absence of sleeping numbers, (and those behaving averagely, which I wanted to ignore as being of no help), there had to be some of them making up for earlier absences. If, therefore, my columns told me that a selection of numbers had been underperforming in my presence, couldn't I expect that at least some of them would compensate in my presence? Surely not a silly assumption?

One novel aspect of the idea was that I could switch between several tables at the same casino, could change casinos, could have a week's rest and carry on from where I had broken off. I was dealing only with what numbers were being spun while I was taking part in a game, (or merely writing them down), regardless of its length and location. And yes, at first I was exclusively chasing sleepers; albeit by instalments.

Referring only to the neighbours listed in my columns, I saw that three numbers, 7 (28/29), 13 (27/36) and 18 (22/29), had yielded no winners at all, and five numbers, (4, 6, 10, 30 and 0), had produced no more than one winner each.

Because of the scarcity of opportunities, dependent on the length of ones wait for a qualifying win, I decided that all three numbers in a group, i.e. the number and its immediate neighbours, should be backed every time the chance arose. This would reduce the odds against a win to only 12/1 but would require an early win, or, say two wins within 20 spins, to make a modest profit. In fact, I was aiming for better than that. These were the results from those eight columns after they had all come up 43 more times:-

```
4  -- 3 wins (1st on 15th spin, 2nd on 17th spin)
6  -- 4 wins (1st on 16th, 2nd on 17th)
7  -- 6 wins (1st on 4th, 2nd on 6th)
10 -- one win on 2nd spin.
13 -- 3 wins (1st on 10th, 2nd on 14th)
18 -- 4 wins (1st on 6th, 2nd on 14th)
```

30 -- 4 wins (1st on 11th, 2nd on 15th)
0 -- 3 wins (1st on 17th, 2nd on 20th)

Eight columns of 43 would have meant 344 spins in which I could make three bets each time, a total outlay of £1,032. How much would the casino expect to win? At 2.7% it works out at just under £28. My figures show £24, which is very close to the theoretical calculation. What does that prove? It proves how SILLY you or I would have been to bet throughout those 344 spins. After all, our hope and intention was to win money, wasn't it? So now take a closer look at those results.

Even the "failure", No.10, offered you £30 clear profit by the second spin.
No.4 made £21 by the 17th spin.
No.7 made £24 by the 4th; and another £30 in two more.
No.13 was £6 in front by the 10th, and £30 by the 14th.
No.18 was £18 up by the 6th and £30 by the 14th.
No.30 had made only £3 by the 11th, but £27 by the 15th.
Zero was still losing £15 after the first win on the 17th spin, but had won £12 by the 20th spin.

Those figures cover many betting-sessions, but clearly every number created its own profit. Had you accepted the quick gain from No.10 and backed the others to a second win, I calculate a profit of 70% on outlay. This is not to say that because of hindsight I am suggesting that you ought to have taken the almost instant profit on No.10. Remember that this didn't happen all at once. Some losses might have been subsidised by other profits, and I look on this sort of thing as a kind of team-effort, (a gamblers' unit trust), in which both losers and winners are to be expected. If I advise you to take out the winners as they happen, not only may you miss other wins, but you could end up with losers only; subject to the proviso that there might always be fresh qualifiers to add to the exercise.

What I do think is that you should have been willing to deal with that collection of numbers in such a way as to pocket a reasonable gain from them. Profit is the name of the game, and profit there certainly was. As for No. 10, you would have been wise to keep <u>some</u> of that £30. No.10's future life produced intermittent wins but it was a long time before its day came. Then it had six wins out of 20; an unsurprising readjustment.

This is another instance where you can take control. Although at one time there may not be many to choose from, there is no need to back every qualifying column. For example at the bottom of my page 6, every number had won 259 times and the expectation was that each number and neighbours would have won 21 times. No.6 was "owing" seven wins and so were Nos.10 and 31. No.24 had recorded 16 wins and therefore owed five, as did 36, but these five were the only ones noticeably below average. No.8 was 11 above average, and No.12 was seven above. "Hot" columns.

I thought of recommending dropping out the winning neighbour of the three and continuing with the other two, but surely it would be painful to see that winner registering its claim a second and more times, as it compensated, unbacked... I turned over the page and saw that No.36 won and nineteen chances later came up three times in a row. On balance it looks best to judge progress on the basis of profit and loss. By the same criterion you can decide whether to raise stakes when winning.

I don't think I have been kidding myself. If I have, I am kidding you too unless you aren't taking the bait, but so far the Silly System, despite its name, is winning good money. If it has to bear the stigma of a number-chasing system, it has a vital defensive quality in that its "chasing" is restricted to the average of three bets for every 37 spins per qualifying number. This means that while pursuing No.1 and its neighbours, 20 and 33, you bet only as often as you see No.1 win. That can't be too often -- unless you intend to start at 2pm and stay until closing-time at 4am, to coincide with the milk round.

Less marathon-minded players, content with a few hours' play, can review at home any threatened danger and if necessary suspend action on all or part of the system. Regard it as your servant, not your master. It is a far different thing seeing ten three-chip losing bets in a whole afternoon or evening, from counting up the result of doggedly backing a "birthday" number which has with equal doggedness remained absent.

In short, although a player might be carried away either in the belief that a number "must" come up or in an over-optimistic attempt to recover painful losses, the Silly System follower is restricted by scarce or missing numbers at any session. Yet an unexpected bonus might arrive should a system qualifier which had thrown up too many losses nevertheless won as a hot number.

You cannot expect all your numbers to be profitable within a given period of time, and some, in isolation, might run up bad losses. Except, obviously, that only one number can win from any spin of the wheel, your numbers are not in competition with one another. Rather, they tend to form a mutually supportive team. If we have a profit, it shouldn't matter to us where it comes from or what the losses are, so long as we can bank the money.

It is best to limit your group to six or eight numbers. Seeing an overall profit (although not automatically as stop-at-a-win), you can cancel the whole group and create a new one. If you take out all the winners, you are left only with losers, so retire both winning _and_ losing numbers for an acceptable net profit. Walk away with your gains and the episode is complete. Don't speculate about what happens behind your back. I record on separate cards each number in play and withdraw them all together. Having written off its loss, you can immediately re-introduce a losing number at nil into a new group, and remember the continually replenished source of qualifying numbers, whether neighbours or not, indicated to follow any other number. You are determined to insist that they're all nothing but 36/1 chances? Yes, admittedly they are, but when you have seen enough hot numbers winning soon enough, (four wins in about 30 spins or even fewer), you may feel far less inhibited by thoughts of 36/1 chances, mathematicians notwithstanding! In due time you may decide that I chose too derogatory a title for this somewhat laborious but apparently moneyspinning scheme.

CHAPTER 10

MANAGING YOUR MONEY.

In a book devoted to the acquisition of money, it would be remiss not to offer some suggestions about ways of looking after it when it had been wrested from the reluctant opposition; increasing it; and, every bit as importantly, protecting it from various forms of attrition. As I have probably made clear, I can see no justification for making a disproportionate splash because you have just won some of "their" money. In the first place it might be no more than some of your own money that you have managed to regain in reduction of previous losses. Secondly, if that were not the case, why shouldn't you now treasure your winnings as _your_ money and treat them and it with proper respect?

One of the weaknesses I have discovered in having a number of different methods is the tendency to try to work them all, out of one more or less unspecified capital sum. This can prove a serious mistake because on the day they choose to be mutually intransigent, you are likely to reach the point where you need to lay out an equal sum on the next three spins and are left with only enough for one of them. Sure as eggs, that is when the second or third spin will throw up the winner, followed by the second winner you should also have had. Now you leave the casino metaphorically broke, when you should have recovered all your losses and perhaps gone on to better things. Yes, I learnt my lesson. Once was enough. Don't let it happen to you -- even once. If, for whatever reason, your betting capital is limited, cut your coat accordingly and decide in advance what method or methods you will be able to afford to operate. Not to do so relinquishes one of your few advantages.

The first thing to realise is that all your forward planning must be done quietly, away from the casino. Trying to scramble out of trouble by changing horses in mid stream, let alone in mid battle, is courting trouble. You know what your maximum available capital is. I don't, so I cannot accurately recommend your best course. I don't know whether you will be pushed to cover just one method, or whether you have ample to bet as flamboyantly as you care to. When you have decided, make sure that you award _each_ _one_ whatever amount of capital you consider to be prudent; and don't be afraid to err on the side of caution. So now let's look at some of the options.

1. Here I am, deciding on the day's action before setting out for a casino. My usual plan is first to play the even chances, (see page 35). Am I going to a casino where I can play £2 stakes? If so, would I be likely to go to a second table if I lost at the first one? As I know that my first three bets could lose, causing me to obey the rule to finish with that system at that table, it is quite possible that I should want to try again at a different one. To cover that eventuality, £20 capital is required for one table and an additional £20 needed for the second one. If I am going to a casino where the minimum bet on the even chances is £5, I must take £50 for each table I think of visiting. Of course I am not forced to _leave_ the table;

only to stop betting in that particular way. By the time the rule operates, whether I am losing or winning, another systematic choice may be available and that would save the inconvenience of trying to find a free space at another table when the casino is crowded. For me, a seat is essential to efficiency and comfort.

2. Quite often my next step after the even chances is to see if the dozens or columns (see page 45), are showing promise, that is to say are clustering together. For this type of play I reckon to have just about £100 to £2 stakes. One problem is that at some tables the equivalent bets on the even and two-to-one chances cannot be made for less than £5 each, and I may deliberately decide to ignore them. In any case whenever there are other bets to make, I tend to leave the columns and dozens out of the calculations. We don't want to get ourselves confused by an overloaded programme. Take the trouble to learn one method thoroughly before attempting to add another one to it.

3. The Foursomes system, (see page 41), is something of a favourite. Because of the waiting-time before possible qualification, I like to play at a minimum stake of £2, which for safety, suggests a capital of up to £400, (obviously proportionately less to a lower stake), but as there wouldn't often be as many as five attempts in my average session of two-and-a-half hours or so, I don't set out with the total capital. Ammunition for a possible five attempts would be sufficient. If these figures cause you misgivings, remember that you could cover a foursome with only two chips, (e.g. 1/4 and 7/10 as splits -- "cheval"), which can be of the minimum value at your table. There's no disgrace in playing low, and until you are experienced and while you are searching for confidence in what you are playing, the less the risk the better.

4. What else do I cater for? Because of its potentially explosive gain, I want to have enough in hand if the sleepers choose to perform for me, (see page 49). The fact that 100 spins have to be seen off makes it most unlikely that more than one opportunity will occur in an afternoon. I now prefer to play this method at £2, making the provision of £28 necessary. All you need is sufficient for 14 stakes at your chosen level because if no win materialises within seven spins, it's a case of waiting for another series of 100 spins or more. Try to summon up the necessary patience. This really is a rewarding system which is quite capable of returning odds of 20/1 to the full amount of money you were willing to risk on it at any one game.

5. Hot numbers, (see page 53), carry the disadvantage of the qualifying time but the advantage of a good percentage return on outlay. At a minimum they are given ten chances of winning at level stakes, but basically it isn't necessary to allow for more than 30 chips at one table. If you can't land a winner in three separate tries, it is better to stop trying at that table. With every method I have recommended it has been a case of hoping to find the favourable trends and of shunning the others.

6. Continuing to back all triple winners, (an improved way of of dealing with double winners: page 53) and increasing stakes

with success, is another rather high risk/high gain method seen as opposing the single wins from following hot numbers -- which sometimes these are. Your own wheel would be a great advantage because this is not a beginner's system to be tried without previous testing. The two pitfalls are when too many numbers qualify and when they are backed for too long after they have qualified. It is most necessary to have a sensible stop-loss point as well as to restrict numbers to perhaps five at a time. You hope that a few numbers will run away from the others. Some days, when they don't, you can be swamped by the numbers which win only twice, and you then have no option but to stop as soon as the danger shows.

On the positive side, considerable profit can be made from a cluster of winning numbers. On the negative, especially with increased stakes, gains can disappear rapidly. Keep this method in reserve until you are completely familiar with the casino and its workings, and even then play it at the lowest possible stakes. I hesitate to be dogmatic about the capital needed, but I think its total might be £250 to cover 50p stakes. Never overlook the principle that our primary concern when facing those challenging odds is SURVIVAL. Lose your capital and you are out of business.

So now, having planned your course of action, which I am sure you will see that at first you must sensibly limit in order to save unnecessary loss; having earmarked sufficient capital, and firmly decided on the point at which to cut your losses, what are you going to do when you realise that you are winning money? This is where your first crucial test emerges. No small part of that test will be to overcome greed.

The great problem connected with winning money at Roulette is the balancing between your optimistic feeling that not only may the same system win for you again but that one of the other systems will also win, and the cautious protection of the money you have won. If you are sitting on what you think of as a nice profit; this being an individual's personal estimate; you should have no problem. You are going away with *most* of that profit, aren't you? Even if you decide to carry on with £20, £30, £50 or whatever else, that is going to be only the smaller portion of your profit. If it isn't, and you dare to leave as a loser, you are fully entitled, and indeed should be compelled, to award yourself the "Supreme Champion Mug" medal.

You cannot expect all your systems to come up trumps on the same day even though they may. What you should try to aim for is the mental attitude that tells you it doesn't matter at all what contributed to your win. If you are money in hand and it is reasonably satisfactory, that is when to set about protecting it. At the same time guard against interpreting this as advice to stop at a win, a concept referred to in Chapter 1. One of the most brilliant International Bridge players of his day, S.J. Simon, wrote in his book, "Why You Lose at Bridge" that a modest professional who invariably stopped as soon as he had won £1, had picked on the stupidest possible system because it meant always turning his back on his luck but deliberately forcing himself to play longer and longer only when he was losing, a fact which contributed to further losses through the faulty judgment of despair. So at Roulette, stay while your profits increase, certainly defend most of them, but don't assume too early that there is no more joy to come.

FOR RICHER FOR POORER?

Whatever the other attractions of gambling, there is no way of excluding the money element. You might suppose that rather in the manner of the youth in that old play, "Love On the Dole," who won a 6d treble (or was it a 3d treble?), on the horses, poorer people or those who strive to be better-off, would be the ones exclusively trying to turn the odds in their favour. Not so. Whether they are entitled to the definition "rich", or whether they just behave in that way, there are plenty of people continually laying out comparatively large amounts of money even in ordinary casinos, and, however many the reverses, seem always able to buy fresh supplies of chips and to do so without ever becoming unruffled in the slightest way when they continue to lose.

If the reports are correct, some of the high-rolling customers, especially those from the oil-rich Middle-east, not only could feel no benefit whatever from a massive win, (that is, massive by most people's standards), but would have the means to buy up a casino or two for themselves. So we should need to enquire from them what it was that gave them satisfaction from gambling. As with any other punter, it could hardly be the lure of easy money, for easy money it certainly isn't in the battle with a casino. Is it perhaps the fact that they know the casino must win which challenges their ego and gives them some feeling of pride on any occasion when they are successful?

It wasn't at Roulette but I have in mind the man who laid out three £1,000 chips, (a split and double), at our £1 Blackjack table, lost to the dealer's unexpected 21, shrugged and walked away. If the gossip was true, that added only about an eighth to his afternoon's losses at Punto Banco. Even that is small beer contrasted with occasional Press reports of pre-arranged casino sessions at which millions rather than thousands have changed hands.

In our case, it surely is the hope, and even the expectation, of beating the odds, making ourselves winners, and at the bottom end of the scale at least being able to pay for a holiday or two in the sun, or, if we prefer that sort of thing, a trip to the Arctic Circle.

WHY "WE" LOSE

Throughout the book, "mathematicians" have been thought of as an anonymous group whose opinions agree as a result of a common understanding of their subject. Accordingly their conclusions warn us that "in the end" we must lose in any situation where we lack a positive expectation of gain, i.e. an advantage, however small, over a casino, a bookmaker, or a machine. An American, Dr. Edward O. Thorp, formerly a professor of mathematics at California University, had by the early 1960s discovered how to obtain an edge over the casino at Blackjack and eventually made so much money by its use that he was banned from playing in all the casinos in Nevada. By then, he had written a book detailing his somewhat complicated methods.

From his student days Dr. Thorp had been interested in the arithmetic of gambling and had spent some years investigating the mechanics of the Roulette wheel. In the course of explaining that every possible gambling system had to fail if the series of bets had a negative expectation, (my suggestion that if it couldn't win on level stakes it couldn't win at all), he wrote that there were only two ways of winning at Roulette. One was from a biased wheel, (but how do you locate it?), and the other by physical prediction. That may well be possible in a laboratory, but you can hardly attempt to transport computers, timing devices and suchlike into a casino!

As expected, he attempted to make no concession whatever to any grouping of similar numbers or patterns, but fixed his attention on the 36/1, (37/1 in the U.S.A.) chance offered by every fresh spin, and although agreeing that some bets are less unwise than others, pronounced that anyone continuing to bet was almost certain to be a loser, eventually stay a loser forever, and finally lose his total capital. Hence the wry joke, "How to make a small fortune at the casino. Go with a large fortune."

Every bet we make at Roulette will be likely to offend the principles laid down by Dr. Thorp, but for the reasons already explained, we may find that we are taking advantage of an edge which he would not acknowledge to be there. I also had in mind that punters in casinos extensively break what are no more than commonsense rules. Here, to illustrate what I mean, are the better ways of getting rid of your money in the fastest time:-

(a) Spreading 20 or more chips at random over the layout, supposing it to be a safer way to wager, for after all you have a good chance of hitting a number. If you do trap the right number your return is no more than one-and-three-quarters times your 20 outlay. If you miss, you are down 20.

(b) Doggedly, session after session backing No.17, or your birthday date or house number. Alternatively, chasing a number which surely is due because it hasn't come up all the evening. Remember sleepers?

(c) Backing the second dozen with increasing stakes because it hadn't come up for ten spins. Can't you see that the other two dozens are really enjoying themselves and aren't ready to give up yet?

(d) Heavily overstaking because of a win, but more especially when hoping to regaining losses.

(e) Disregarding any of the safety rules attaching to the various recommended methods you have been offered.

Those should be enough warnings to last you a lifetime.

CHAPTER 11

CROOKED WHEEL? FORGET IT!

Apart from the fact that punters themselves make it quite unnecessary for casino operators to think up possible ways of cheating, and apart too, from the danger of being closed down by the Gaming Board should illegalities be discovered, the opportunities are not too obvious. In the case of Blackjack the four packs of cards are thoroughly shuffled together and are then cut by one of the players. They are placed face down in a dealing-box or "shoe", from which they are dealt one at a time. Even if the dealer were able to identify certain cards, he has no control over the number of cards drawn by players under the rules. He handles only one card at a time, all are dealt face up (in the United Kingdom), dealers change tables every so often, have no discretion about the number of cards they may draw for their own hands, and in short, the possibility of cheating is remote. At Blackjack, punters may average a 25% loss by their universally bad play, so why try card-marking?

Fresh cards are used every day, the old ones being mechanically shredded. I once asked whether anyone had thought of giving a few packs to hospitals for the entertainment of convalescing patients, but the opinion seemed to be that the cards had to be destroyed. With the numbers involved, I then envisaged a hospital buried in cards from a regular daily supply.

I have no first hand experience of playing Blackjack in America, but it is usually understood that originally the game could be played one-to-one with a single pack of cards which was held in the dealer's hand. In those circumstances I'm sure we all know from card-manipulation shown on television that anything would be possible. Going back thirty years, as soon as some players demonstrated their capability of counting the number of vital cards already dealt and instantaneously calculating the odds from the remaining cards, the casinos were forced to make the game more complicated for those "counters" by increasing the number of packs of cards in use for each deal. This made a dealing shoe virtually indispensable and that surely restricted the opportunities for card-palming. I cannot say "eliminated" in view of the fact that the dealer handles all the cards when shuffling. I have referred to Blackjack because it is one of several casino games all of which come under the umbrella of the Gaming Board, which naturally enough does its utmost to ensure honest play on the part of both dealer and casino.

Blackjack played in one of the unlicensed and therefore illegal casinos about which there are reports from time to time, might result in your facing a dealer manipulating a single pack. But if you choose to enter a "clip-joint" how can you expect not to be fleeced?

Is Roulette cheat-proof? There is a perhaps surprisingly large number of people who are convinced that a dealer can "spin" whatever number he chooses. I once heard a player ask the dealer what the next number would be. "Put your rent-money on 5," the dealer said, and to his amused, semi-embarrassment spun

15. It was of course absolute coincidence. The other coincidence was that no player, including the enquirer, had put a single chip on that No.15.

At one casino, I witnessed a genuinely angry man arguing at length that every spin at Roulette was planned by the management. "They," he shouted, pointing upwards to where the video cameras were situated, "tell him," stabbing a finger towards the smiling croupier, "exactly which number to bring up." This caused a burst of laughter from the staff and players alike, and the reply from the croupier, "Yes, sir, it's how I made my first million." The man's convictions weren't to be shaken, and he stormed out, calling, "It's crooked, crooked, crooked. I'll never come here again!"

It seems possible, in this advanced technological age, that a computer-controlled wheel with a computer-driven ball might combine to settle a ball into a nominated slot. For a human being to achieve such a thing is quite beyond belief. We are considering a mechanical situation where a millimetre can make the difference between one slot and another, (even extending to opposite sides of the wheel), where an impossible degree of co-ordination would be required. The wheel is gently impelled in one direction. No two "pushes" could be that precisely identical, so the wheel must spin at variable speeds. The ball is projected at different strengths, sometimes because an obliging croupier makes it a long spin at the request of a player. At the beginning of every spin the croupier has to take the ball from the last winning slot, reverse the wheel, and send the ball in the opposite direction. Suppose he took the ball from slot 30 and decided he would try for 33. His estimate has to embrace exactly seven slots on the wheel. So, discounting all those metal projections intended to divert the path of the moving ball, the calculation of place, momentum and micro-timing are quite absurdly impossible for a human being to achieve.

Even if there were a "controller" above the table to send messages to the croupier by some form of undetectable microphone, how could success still be ensured? At a late point in the betting, by which time there are frequently massses of chips spread about the table, the controller sees no chips on No.1. "Spin one" he orders. The croupier obeys, brilliantly calculating the number of intervening slots and adjusting everything necessary to achieve his target. The ball has completed a number of circuits of the wheel. Players are still laying out chips. "No more bets," the croupier calls for the first time. Bets continue to be laid. "That's all, thank you. No more bets," the croupier finally announces. Clever man. No.1 wins. So does the jubilant punter who, just in time, bet the maximum on it.

The logical ending to this piece of fantasy would be the revelation that the placer of the winning bet was a well-known electronics wizard, (Chairman of a multi-national computer Company?), who had found a way of tuning in to the transmitted messages, so making a fortune for himself, and in every sense beating the casino at its own game. No, I don't think we should allow ourselves to be inhibited by the fears of miracles being performed against us.

I have heard it suggested, mainly in support of the "neighbours" theory, that an experienced, or a tired croupier will tend to spin in an automatic way which lands the ball into or close to its previous slot. It is true that at times it is noticeable how many neighbours; especially those in the next slot to the preceding one; are turning up. "He's spinning nothing but neighbours," they'll tell one another at the table. By now, you know enough about the trends at Roulette to accept that this could be put down to a compensatory phase after a dearth of neighbour-spinning. Have you also supposed that all these neighbours were clustered together in a particular section of the wheel, and that it must be the result of the croupier's special touch?

In a matter of 15 spins or less, you might see 9-22-9, (next to each other), 23-8, (next), and 21-21-2, (a repeat and a next-slot winner), but are these in a bunch? They are not. 23 is 11 slots away from 22; 23 is 12 slots away from 21; and 21 is 14 slots from 22. This is another example of the symmetry of the wheel. So although these are undeniably neighbours, they aren't neighbours of neighbours, and you would have to find a different explanation from that of a clever or tired croupier. There is a further objection. A new croupier, working the first week of a new career, and very obviously a beginner, is just as likely as his seniors to produce spin after spin in the same quarter of the wheel, and serve you a helping of neighbours regardless of your interest in that particular form of wagering. There is no, repeat, no, more reason for the next winning number to be that of the slot next to the present number than it is to be exactly on the opposite side of the wheel. Neighbours are often "noticed" because people are looking for them, yet you are unlikely to see anyone counting up the number of spins since two neighbouring numbers occurred. At Roulette "everything" happens and every number follows every other number, including itself. Infinity neatly balances them all and certainly doesn't give preference to neighbours, so when they occur, singly or in groups, it is just that it is their turn to do so. Try to avoid the habit of regarding them as a standardised bet.

No, please let's forget all about neighbours and particularly about gifted croupiers. Accept that whatever you see is at worst coincidence and at best no more than the manifestation of the inevitable cyclic behaviour of that entirely random wheel. Make sure that when you walk out of a casino, it is not angrily because of some illogical superstitious confrontation, but more likely because you have some of "their" money stuffed into your pocket.

In my experience, the nearest a casino comes to cheating is when, say, a known system-player who tends to be successful, finds that a dealer shortens the time between spins in an attempt to fluster the punter and prevent him from placing all the bets his system requires. Your answer to this sort of conduct is to ask for longer time in which to make your bets, and if he continues to gallop on, you can gently protest to the supervisor. The alternative is to cash your chips and move to another table. In the main, they will do as you ask. I told one young lady that I hadn't come to the casino to take part in a race. In this instance I was alone at the table, but she slowed down with perfectly good grace.

Can we class fast spinning as cheating? Not in the hard, competitive world where there are doubtless somewhat easier places from which to obtain money than in casinos. The quicker they can get the tables covered with chips, and the wheel spinning, the quicker they can rake in their profit. Incidentally it is only in French-type Roulette that chips are literally raked in. You will usually see in what is called American Roulette, (although, thankfully, the double-zero is missing), that the dealer, using only his clasped hands, sweeps the losing chips into a hole in the table. There, an electronic device quickly sorts them into their various colours for immediate future use.

It could be argued that the American wheel with its 0 and 00 (which share the space on the layout), represents blatant, legalised cheating, for now, instead of playing against 2.7%, you face the payment of 35/1 for a 37/1 chance; a handicap of over 5.2%. My methods can win against it, but it is so <u>greedy!</u> My American friend says that he would never play the even chances against their wheel.

Classed in part with inefficiency is the possibility of being cheated in the amount of a payout or the number of chips handed over in exchange for cash. The remedy is simple! You just need to calculate the amount of your win and to check the number of chips you ought to receive for your money. If a croupier is inexperienced and possibly nervous, he can of course miscalculate. If he is an old hand and a little slapdash by overconfidence, he may also make mistakes, but the supervisor's duty is to check that payments are correct -- and not least on behalf of the casino to prevent staff from overpaying someone with whom they might have had an "arrangement". Any consistent under payment to punters would soon cause acid comments from the players themselves, so that deliberate short-changing would be carried out, as it were, under the guns of the enemy.

In assuring you of the safeguards to prevent cheating in the United Kingdom, naturally enough I cannot offer a worldwide guarantee that nowhere is there a casino effectively controlled by a greedy criminal organisation. In that case there may be punters at additional risk, but because casinos are such valuable money-generators which obviously attract close attention from interested governments, the majority of casinos must be subject to stringent supervision. No doubt any closed because of corruption would be quickly reopened under new management.

CHAPTER 12

BETTING STRATEGY SUMMARISED AS QUESTION AND ANSWER

Question. You tell me to protect my profit. Should I stop at a win?

Answer. No. Certainly not as a habit. To do so keeps you at the table through all the losing spells but allows you no winnng runs. If it happened that you had played for a long time without much progress, but then when it was approaching the time for you to leave the casino your number came up, you might feel quite happy to stop at that win.

Question. Am I ever justified in exceeding my stop-loss?

Answer. You now tread dangerous ground. The loss-limit is for your own protection -- largely from yourself. Once you think of it as optional, it might as well not be there. I would allow only one exception. If I were following a method with a specific number of bets which had not yet been completed, I should want to finish that series, for better or worse.

Question. If I did continue, and won, what then?

Answer. Although you may still be a net loser, you will have drawn back from the stop-loss position, and that would allow you to continue betting. You would need to check whether you had reached a stop-loss point in relation to a particular system. If so, it would be wrong to use your winnings simply to go on past your warning-sign. On the other hand there might be a winning opportunity from another method. You would need still to keep an eye on the overall loss limit. Don't try to cheat. Why would you want to cheat yourself?

Question. If I am winning, how do I know when I ought to stop?

Answer. With all casino gaming, there is no point in going away while your winnings continue to mount up. It is the situation people might pray for. Where you need to be excessively cautious is when those winnings begin to dribble away. So keep going until it turns sour for you, and make sure you "get going" very soon after that. The point about a winning run is that you are probably riding a wavy line. You cannot know when, or whether, there will be another win, or, if there is to be one, how long you may have to wait for it. While waiting, you will necessarily be making losing bets and the curve will be dropping from the previous peak. If you feel you might not trust your will or your judgment at the table, it would be best to make a rule beforehand. Some financial experts advise selling company Shares if they drop by 10%. For the casino, I would prefer 20% but not more than 25%, and there is no reason at all why you shouldn't carry a little chart with you for instant guidance when you are in doubt. For instance, 20% down from £30 is £24; from £50 is £40; from £100 is £80. 25% down from £30 is £22.50 (up to £23 or down to £22); from £50 is £37.50 (up to £38 or down to £37); and of course from £100 is £75. If you rise beyond a previous peak, your quitting-point must rise with it just as with Shares, when you would revise your stop-loss with every advance in price.

Question. If I do well, is it advisable to increase the value of my basic stake?

Answer. The quick reply is yes, but there is a very important two-part answer to this question. If you double your capital, you could double your stakes. If you increase your capital by a half, you could do the same with your stakes unless you were betting in a way which only allowed for a whole-number stake. With sufficient gain, you could increase stakes in one system despite having won the money on a different one. There is a clear choice of options. What you must do is keep your increases in absolute proportion to the amount you have won. Don't, if you have doubled your capital, increase your stakes to three times their original value. Far rather, wait until you had trebled your capital before doubling the stake. If you felt really cautious, you could raise your stakes by steps which always increased the distance between outlay and capital. That could create a nice cushion between you and disaster. Never forget that survival is paramount.

Now to the equally important second part of the answer. If you are battling it out on minimum stakes and keep losing, you have nowhere to drop. The alternative to fighting on is to give up. It is, though, only fair to yourself and your capital, to allow the system to justify itself. After all, that was the whole point of putting the capital together in the first place. It is a different matter if after you have raised your stakes you then begin to lose. At some point you must lower your stakes again. This should no more be done in panic than the raising should have been bounced up optimistically. It surely makes sense that if your capital drops back to the point at which you raised your stakes you certainly should return them to the original amount, but there is a more prudent way of doing it.

When deciding to increase your stakes, your task should be at the same time to fix the point at which you will drop them to their former level if you run into losses. As a rough guide, I suggest the loss of 12.5% (one-eighth) of your new, i.e. increased, capital should put you into retreat. This would mean that if you were playing £1 stakes to a £100 capital you would increase to £2 stakes when the capital reached £200, but that you would revert to £1 stakes when the capital dropped back to £175. Conversely, if that lost £25 were subsequently recovered, you should restore £2 stakes. Be particularly careful to guard against drastic reductions through panic. Divide your stakes by four, and it will take four times as long for your wins to bring you to recovery, therefore, resolve that both increases and decreases are kept to your previously-decided ratio. Throughout the book you have been warned of the need for self-discipline. No other way is safe; or at least every other way is less safe.

That ends our journey to the doors of the casino. To any of you brave enough to enter, I can but offer the wish that all your favourable trends are lengthy ones and that the timing of your arrival at a chosen gaming-table, is happily selected.

======

APPENDIX 1

"Talking-through" a session played on 23.3.1989, at which the even chances and dozens/columns were at minimum £5. The scorecards at the casinos I visit restrict me to 3" of writing-space so entries must necessarily be <u>very</u> condensed. Because you will be faced with the same problem, I hope you will study my abbreviations so that you understand and can use them yourself. Remember, they were explained in full on page 46 of Chapter 6. I cannot, for example, afford the luxury of "13d/2W" to indicate that the first and third dozens were backed for two units each and won. I write that as 13² and use a tiny x or tick for loss or win. Nor can I afford "B/5*L" to indicate Black backed for 5 units (* the alternation between Black and Red), which lost. Before the result, it is entered as B5*. Most of the time I use the first three printed columns for entering the number, dozen and column of that number; for example 27 3 C (27, 3rd dozen and 3rd column), and that leaves me a mere one and three-quarters of an inch for all the rest of my entries.

In order to reduce the confusion, I have omitted classification of the columns (ABC), and in the hope of making the bets clearer, I have often introduced diagonal spacers for which there is no room in practice. Normally, that first bet, O/5L would indicate a £5 losing bet on Zero. In this case it is £5 on Odd (O5x on my scorecard), which lost to Even. The bets begin after the first two qualifying numbers, 27 and 29:-

```
27 (3rd dozen)
29 (3)
34 (3)      bets:       O/5L      H/5W                       --    --
1  (1)      B/5*L                 H/10L                      x    (15)
       (Note that the four results have all fallen
        within the first and third dozens. A trend?
        Try them at £2 each)
10 (1)      R5L         E/5*W                     13d/2W     x    (13)
5  (1)                  O/10*W    L/5W            13d/2W     W     4
11 (1)      B/5*W       E/20*L    L/10W           13d/2W     x     1
6  (1)      R/10*L                L/20W           13d/2W     W    13
15 (2)      B/5W                  L/25W           13d/2L     W    39
16 (2)      B/10L       E/5*W     L/30W           12d/2W     W    66
17 (2)                  O/10*W    L/35W           12d/2W     W   113
16 (2)      R/5*W       E/20*W    L/40W           12d/2W     W   180
22 (2)      B/10*W      O/25*L    L/45L           12d/2W     x   122
34 (3)      R/20*W      E/5W                      12d/2L     W   143
6  (1)      B/25*W      E/10W     H/5L            23d/2L     W   169
11 (1)      R/30*L      E/20L                                x   119
       (When the stakes begin to mount up, there must
        always be a biggish drop when the loss occurs.
        From a high point of 180, now is the time for
        caution).
11 (1)      B/5W                  L/5W                       W   129
23 (2)      B/10L       O/5W      L/10L                      x   114
36 (3)                  O/10L                                x   104
25 (3)      R/5W                  H/5W                       W   114
7  (1)      R/10W       E/5*L     H/10L                      x   109
14 (1)      R/20W       O/5L                                 W   124
7  (1)      R/25W                 L/5W                       W   154
```

0	0	R/30	E/5*L	L/10L	(half)	x	131
5	(1)	R/15W	E/5*L	L/5W		W	146
21	(2)	R/20W	O/5W	L/10L		W	161
28	(3)	R/25L	O/10L	L/20L		x	105
			(Nasty! Last try)				
36	(3)			H/5W		W	110
21	(3)	B/5*L	E/5L	H/10W		--	110
34	(3)	R/5W		H/20W		w	135
25	(3)	R/10W	O/5*W	H/25W		W	176
32	(3)	R/20W	E/10*W	H/30W		W	235
17	(2)	R/25L	O/20*W	H/35L		x	195
3	(1)		E/25L			x	170
16	(2)	B/5*L	O/5L	L/5W		x	165

THREE CONSECUTIVE LOSSES. No more even-chances' play. Absolutely no bad marks awarded if you had decided to stop earlier at plus £104. Now there is an alternation on the dozens:

11	(1)	13d/2*W		W	167
29	(3)	23d/2*W		W	169
8	(1)	12d/2*W		W	171
26	(3)	13d/2W		W	173
7	(1)	12d/2*W		W	175
4	(1)	23d/2*L		W	171

This is a good point at which to look at the frequency of wins of individual numbers. In the first 31 spins nine numbers won twice, and two, Nos. 11 and 34 had won three times. In the next ten spins two more numbers won twice; obviously too many to be handled if you intended backing that category. If you waited for the three-times' winners, No.11 had achieved this by the 16th spin, (and won again 20 spins later), No.34 won for the third time on spin 30, joined by No.16 on the 35th spin and by No.7 on the 40th spin. Watch these as the numbers continue:

7	(1)	Fourth win.			
17	(1)	Third win.			
10	(1)	Second win.			
24	(2)				
29	(3)	Third win.			
11	(1)	Fifth win, on rising stakes.			
16	(2)	Fourth win on rising stake.			
31	(3)				
26	(3)				
29	(3)	4th. win: three in 15 spins and HOT, so continue to back it for ten spins in any case.			
19	(2)	29/1L		x	170
28	(3)	29/1L		x	169
11	(1)	29/1L	No.11 sixth win!	x	168
3	(1)	29/1L		x	167
17	(2)	29/1L	No.17 fourth win	x	166
20	(2)	29/1L		x	165
28	(3)	29/1L	No.28 third win	x	164
13	(2)	29/1L		x	163

```
35  (3)    29/1L                                               x   162
 2  (1)    29/1L                                               x   161
```

End of hot No. bets but 29 could still
be backed with the other three-timers.
FOURSOMES. It is 33 spins since one of
the numbers 27-30-33-36 won. Keep watch.
Pick up alternation on dozens.

```
24  (2)    23d/2*W                                             W   163
32  (3)    13d/2*W                                             W   165
13  (2)    12d/2*W                                             W   167
31  (3)    13d/2*W                                             W   169
26  (3)    12d/2*L    End of alternation on dozens.            x   165
12  (1)    23d/2L                                              x   161
 8  (1)
 6  (1)    13d/2W                                              W   163
 9  (1)    13d/2W                                              W   165
 9  (1)    13d/2W                                              W   167
34  (3)    13d/2W                                              W   169
17  (2)    13d/2L                                              x   165
27  (3)           Foursome. Cheapest bet, 3 chips.
15  (2)    27/1, 27-30/1, 33-36/1                              x   162
21  (2)    27/1, 27-30/1. 33-36/1                              x   159
33  (3)    27/1, 27-30/1, 33-36/1W                             W   174
```

Now you wish you had put on 2-1-1-1 chips
but try for one more win in three spins:

```
23  (2)    27/1, 27-30/1, 33-36/1                              x   171
24  (2)    27/1, 27-30/1, 33-36/1                              x   168
12  (1)    27/1, 27-33/1, 33-36/1                              x   165
```
FOURSOME. Nos. 1-4-7-10 qualified. Watch.

```
 5  (1)    12d/2W                                              W   167
13  (2)    12d/2W                                              W   169
 3  (1)    12d/2W                                              W   171
25  (3)    12d/2L                                              x   167
33  (3)
 3  (1)
36  (3)
 2  (1)
27  (3)    33, 36 and 27 (previous foursome), win
           within five spins.

 1  (1)    New Foursome to back.
 4  (1)    1/1  1-4/1W  7-10/1  (immediate win)                W   182
29  (3)    1/1  1-4/1   7-10/1                                 x   179
26  (3)    1/1  1-4/17-10/1                                    x   176
 1  (1)    1/1W, 1-4/1W, 7-10/1  wins 51 chips,                W   227
           35 "straight up" plus 17 on the
           1/4 split, less 7/10 loser.
           Stop at this second win.

27  (3)    Notice 13 successive wins in 1st-3rd dozens.
 2  (1)    96 spins gone and only two numbers (18 & 30)
           remain sleeping.
16  (2)
```

0	0						
3	(1)						
3	(1)						
30	(3)	SLEEPER. Won on 101st spin. Back 18 & 30 for up to seven spins.					
15	(2)	18/1	30/1	spin	(1)	x	225
11	(1)	18/1	30/1 (next, but no pay!)		(2)	x	223
15	(2)	18/1	30/1		(3)	x	221
13	(2)	18/1	30/1		(4)	x	219
30	(3)	18/1	30/1W		(5)	W	253
		Double stakes for up to 7 spins.					
3	(1)	18/2	30/2		(1)	x	249
31	(3)	18/2	30/2		(2)	x	245
10	(1)	18/2	30/2		(3)	x	241
27	(3)	18/2	30/2		(4)	x	237
36	(3)	18/2	30/2		(5)	x	233
4	(1)	18/2	30/2		(6)	x	229
35	(3)	18/2	30/2		(7)	x	225
		End of session.					

Application of various methods, combined to beat the casino as follows:-
  1. Even chances, won.
  2. Dozens at 2/1, won.
  3. Hot number, lost.
  4. Two foursomes, won.
  5. Sleepers, a part success, losing two units, i.e. lost.
  6. Numbers winning twice only were too numerous and would have had to be curtailed even though No.11 won quickly, and eventually won seven times in 113 spins. Waiting for the three-timers, (11, 34, 16, 7, 17 29, and 28 of the early ones), would have been profitable although not all of them won.

If you ask why I put up with a cramped scorecard instead of providing my own, wider chart, it's because conditions can often be crowded at a table so the least paperwork you have to cope with the better. I manage well enough with a few cards held as a pad in the span of my hand. Another consideration is my conscious attempt to remain inconspicuous. It is perfectly normal to be seen using the casino's cards but I have occasionally noticed someone with a wide, printed card with various headings, and immediately that player has drawn attention to himself as someone who intends to bet in a routine way. Naturally this invites the casino staff to take a closer look, and I think we do best to avoid that as far as possible.

APPENDIX 2

The following spins are the beginning of a long sequence which were recorded many years ago by a journalist at a casino and were offered for system-testing. They illustrate for us how profit can be made while waiting for the final sleepers to mature and themselves contribute their share of profit. Even-chance betting was illustrated in Appendix 1, so although I reserved the possibility of backing the dozens, and have accordingly listed them in brackets, I had "number" methods more in mind.

```
30  (3)
17  (2)
 3  (1)
32  (3)
 9  (1)
19  (2)
23  (2)
17  (2)    2nd win
35  (3)
 6  (1)
13  (2)
 0   0
29  (3)
10  (1)
 7  (1)
14  (2)
```

(No.17 has already won twice. No.14 is next to it on the layout and this would allow us to back those two numbers with a single chip placed on the line between them. It is known as a split, or officially as Carré. The game is of course conducted in English, so you don't have to worry about "Faites vos jeux" or learning to count in French. Note that you wouldn't split No.17 simply because it had won twice, but in this case as No.14 has also won, you know it isn't a sleeper). Continuing:

```
10  (1)   2nd win.  14-17/1x    (add 7/10 split for a         (1)
                                      similar reason)
21  (2)             14-17/1x   7-10/1x                        (3)
 3  (3)   2nd win.  14-17/1x   7-10/1x                        (5)
 1  (1)             14-17/1x   7-10/1x                        (7)
28  (3)             14-17/1x   7-10/1x                        (9)
14  (2)   2nd win   14-17/1W   7-10/1x     Win 16              7
 5  (1)             14-17/2x      "    x   (increase as both   4
                                             won twice)
 4  (1)                "    x      "    x                      1
32  (3)   2nd win      "    x      "    x                     (2)
 7  (1)   2nd win   14-17/2x   7-10/1W     Win 15             13
15  (2)                "    x      "    x                     10
 1  (1)   2nd win      "    x      "    x                      7
                    (add 1/4)
 1  (1)   3rd win   14-17/2x   7-10/1x   1-4/1W   Win 14      21
                    (bet 1, a 3-timer and wait for 4)
10  (1)   3rd win   14-17/2x   7-10/1W   1/1x     Win 14      35
                    (bet 10 and wait for 7)
```

30	(3)	2nd win	14-17/2x	10/1	x	1/1x				31
19	(2)	2nd win	"	x	"	x	"	x		27
15	(2)	2nd win	"	x	"	x	"	x		23
24	(2)		"	x	"	x	"	x		19
23	(2)		"	x	"	x	"	x		15
22	(2)		"	x	"	x	"	x		11
14	(2)	3rd win	14-17/2W	"	x	"	x	Win 32		43
			(bet 14 and wait for 17)							
15	(2)	3rd win	14/1x	10/1x	1/1x					40
			(bring in 15)							
11	(1)		1/1x	10/1	14/1x	15/1x				36
1	(1)	4th win	1/1W	"	x	"	x	"	x	Win 32	68
7	(1)	3rd win	1/2x	"	x	"	x	"	x		63
			(bring in 7)							
11	(1)	2nd win	1/2x	10/1x	14/1x	15/1	7/1x			57

Our primary object in visiting casinos is the unashamed attempt to win money. This we have now achieved and the present commitment is six chips (£6?) a spin. From a maximum of 68, our total winnings could disappear in ten more spins. Greed suggests that these five numbers might double the winnings. Prudence advises stopping -- at any rate at the 50-mark. That allows just one more losing spin. After that we can look for other methods. Currently there have been 11 successive wins between the first and second dozens; something we shall learn to call, simply, "12". So:

21	(2)	2nd win	1/2x	10/1x	14/1x	15/1x	7/1x	51
21	(2)	3rd win, but stop.						
9	(1)							

There are no obvious foursomes, and it might be a little late to step into that 12-sequence. Wait, then, until that run of dozens changes. Meanwhile we aren't losing money.

22	(2)			
29	(3)	Change to 3rd dozen.		
27	(3)			
32	(3)			
14	(2)	Now start with 23² W (2 chips each dozen)	W	53
35	(3)	23² W	W	55
19	(2)	" W	W	57
26	(3)	" W	W	59
12	(1)	" Lose 4	x	55
29	(3)	23²*W Did you read the alternation?	W	57
12	(1)	12²*W	W	59
30	(3)	23²*W	W	61
35	(3)	12²*Lost 4	x	57
19	(2)	13²Lost 4	x	53
32	(3)			
4	(1)			
5	(1)			
16	(2)			
2	(1)			
6	(1)	12²W	W	55
0	0	12²L	x	51
22	(2)	12²W	W	53
25	(3)	12²L	x	49

```
15  (2)
33  (3)
30  (3)   232W                                          W    51
10  (1)   232L                                          x    47
 6  (1)
30  (3)   132W      (4th win for 30)                    W    49
34  (3)   132W                                          W    51
12  (1)   132W                                          W    53
 6  (1)   132W      (4th win for 6)                     W    55
13  (2)   132L                                          x    51
15  (2)
25  (3)   122L                                          x    47
16  (2)
13  (2)   232W                                          W    49
28  (3)   232W                                          W    51
14  (2)   232W                                          W    53
24  (2)   232W                                          W    55
27  (3)   232W                                          W    57
 7  (1)   232L                                          x    53
19  (2)
21  (2)
22  (2)
11  (1)   122W                                          W    55
18  (2)   122W                                          W    57
28  (3)   122L      (2nd win for 28)                    x    53
 3  (1)
11  (1)
 7  (1)
31  (3)   132W                                          W    55
28  (3)   132W      (3rd win for 28: Hot No. Allow up to   W    57
                    10 bets for a win. No dozens-bets).

 6  (1)   28/1L     (5th win for No.6)                  x    56
26  (3)   28/1L     (Just enough time to note the       x    55
                    remaining sleepers: Nos.8, 20 & 36)

18  (2)   28/1L                                          x    54
 7  (1)   28/1L     (next to 28)                         x    53
33  (3)   28/1L                                          x    52
25  (3)   28/1L     (6th spin. Now double stake)         x    51
29  (3)   28/2L                                          x    49
10  (1)   28/2L                                          x    47
28  (3)   28/2W     Joy! Plus 70. Stop that series.      W   117
21  (2)                                                  -   117
 8  (1)             Sleepers: wait for 20 or 36 to win.  -   117
32  (3)
26  (3)             No dozens bet available.
20  (2)   Won on 112th spin. Back 20/36 for up to 7 spins.
19  (2)   20/1x  36/1x          (Spin 1)                 x   115
34  (3)   20/1x  36/1x             "  (2)                x   113
 9  (1)   20/1x  36/1x             "  (3)                x   111
 8  (1)   20/1x  36/1x             "  (4)  (8 again!)    x   109
12  (1)   20/1x  36/1x             "  (5)                x   107
36  (3)   20/1x  36/1 YES          "  (6)                W   141
          Chips in hand, 38, so bet 2 chips on each number
          for up to 7 more spins.
16  (2)   20/2x  36/2x          (Spin 1)                 x   137
32  (3)   20/2x  36/2x             "  (2)                x   133
```

```
32  (3)    20/2x   36/2x                  "    (3)                        x   129
25  (3)    20/2x   36/2x                  "    (4)                        x   125
20  (2)    20/2W   36/2x    Won 68        "    (5)                        W   193
           Chips in hand from this game 88 so bet 6 chips per
                  spin up to seven spins (stop at a win).
12  (1)    20/6x   36/6x              (Spin 1)                            x   181
28  (3)    20/6x   36/6x                  "    2                          x   169
22  (2)    20/6x   36/6x                  "    3                          x   157
21  (2)    20/6x   36/6x                  "    4                          x   145
20  (2)    20/6W   36/6x   YES            "    5        Won 199           W   344
```

The end of a very satisfactory session. At the start, the even chances would have lost your maximum, but each of the other four methods demonstrated, (the dozens, the two- and three-times winners, hot numbers, and the sleepers), contributed to a handsome profit. You will suffer many worse sessions but you may well have better ones. The fact that I arbitrarily announced the end of the session isn't of great importance. You might have continued and won more, or you might have lost, but I could not see myself (nor you, I hope), leaving the casino with less than £300 profit. My sessions rarely last longer than 130 to 150 spins.

You will notice that No.20, the number which brought the sleepers' play into action, was the one winning twice more against the gratefully welcomed win of No.36, so that if you had adopted the option, described on page 50, of backing No.20 more heavily (in the ratio of three to two), than No.36 the profit would have been correspondingly greater. No.20's last win qualified it as a hot number and I haven't shown you that it would have been a loser. My philosophy has been that one winning hot number in a session is a reasonably satisfactory target, even though I back foursomes at every opportunity. Secondly, I cannot remember ever staying on at a table after backing my "Sleeping Partners"; win or lose.

These various examples of ways to beat the casino may have appeared somewhat daunting at first, but a little patient study should soon enable you to add them to your armoury. As a last word, this session did happen, and what a pity neither of us was able to be there to take advantage of it.

=======

APPENDIX 3

If you are going into business, you must of course behave in a businesslike way if you hope to succeed. No apology should therefore be necessary in recommending that you keep a faithful record of all wins and losses, (no cheating, because you won't kid yourself), from your very first session. The great advantage to be gained is the pinpointing of progress, good or bad, for each separate method you choose to follow, and the growing confidence which mounting profit gives you. It also sounds a warning when losses also pile up. Then you have to ask whether you are playing properly, whether the method is as good as you hoped, or is it simply a case of having to ride out a losing run.

Given adequate capital for each method you fancy, it is probably an advantage to follow two or three at a time because they can be mutually supportive. It is rather trying, though, when they all fail together. That is liable to be "chin up" time, but I have to say that I have suffered very little from depressing sequences of that kind. A friend tells me that so often he has seen me do the "Houdini" act almost at the end of a turbulent session.

For your records you need a lined book in which you can rule 3/4" columns. As you can use two pages at a time, a book 5" wide should be suitable. These, in rather cramped form, are most of my headings:-

Date	Even Chances	Dozs. Cols.	Hot Nos.	Four-somes	Sleep-ers	CASINO & stake		Net win/ (lose)
Jan.								
5	(12.00)	18.00	(10.00)	–	–	Gold	£1	(4.00)
8	16.00	4.00	30.00	(18.00)		Gold	£1	28.00
14	24.00	(6.00)	–	24.00		Tulip	£1	70.00
17	(11.00)	(16.00)	(10.00)			Gold	£1	33.00
18	(15.00)	18.00		(9.00)		Gold	£1	17.00
21	(8.00)	8.00		(9.00)		Gold	£1	8.00
23	(6.00)	10.00		53.00		Tulip	£1	65.00
26	(7.00)	4.00	33.00			Tulip	£1	95.00
28	40.00	(6.00)	(10.00)	28.00		Tulip	£1	147.00

and so on... By the way, the amounts shown were taken at random and do not necessarily relate to specific bets made for those individual methods.

There is no need to make your losing entries in red. It is simpler to put brackets round them as I have in the first line: Even Chances losing £12, Hot Numbers losing £10, and total loss on the day £4.

If, as I do, you also play Blackjack, you will need to bring in, after "Casino", extra columns headed "Roulette" and "Blackjack". Clearly, the daily columns of your different methods will have to agree with the total you enter in the "Roulette" column, and if you play Blackjack on the same day, that will have to be taken into account for the final column. The last three columns may now look like this:-

	Roulette	Blackjack	Net win/(lose)
	20.00	--	20.00
	15.00	(20.00)	15.00
	35.00	10.00	60.00
	--	(15.00)	45.00
	(10.00)	30.00	65.00
	18.00	--	83.00
	£78.00	£5.00	

At this stage the totals of the columns for all the separate methods, whether winning or losing, would have to agree with that Roulette total of £78, and you notice that this total added to the Blackjack total agrees with the net plus of £83, and so the "books" balance.

I am sure that this not too arduous extra task will be found to be a great help in the battle. Besides, wouldn't it be nice to be able to flash some figures before the eyes of doubting friends?

INDEX

	Page
ACCOUNT BOOK: for wins and losses	81
ARITHMETIC: bearing on games of chance.	3
distinguish long- and short-term	20
repeating numbers	40
"BEST" WAYS OF LOSING: what to avoid	66
BETTING STRATEGY: question and answer	71
CAPITAL: sufficient is essential	43/62-64
CASINO: has right to ban players for:-	
bad behaviour }	
cheating }	2/3
winning! }	
CHEATING: unlikely by licensed U.K. casinos	16
CHIPS: coloured/money	19
CLASSIFYING NUMBERS: by dozen and column	46/47
COLUMNS AND DOZENS: played at 2/1	45
COIN TOSSING: relationship to even chances	20/34
CROUPIER OR DEALER	19/67/68
DOUBLING UP STAKES: don't	26
DOZENS AND COLUMNS: played at 2/1	45
EVEN CHANCES: and how to back them	20/35
FACING THE ODDS	5
FAST SPINNING	69
FOOTBALL-POOL BETTING: unfavourable odds	14
FOURSOMES, FINDING FAVOURABLE:	41
How to play	42
GAMING ACT: overall control of U.K. gaming	16
GREYHOUND RACING: cramped odds offered	10
GREED: the potential loss-maker	23
HORSE RACING: difficulties to overcome	6
HOT NUMBERS	53
INCREASING STAKES: from profits only	72
LAYOUT	18
MANAGING YOUR MONEY	62
MONTE CARLO	1
NEIGHBOURS (and see Silly System)	57/69
NUMBER "CHASING": don't	3
ODDS:	
(Odd numbers) -- see Even Chances	
Paid for various bets	19
"PIT BOSS": i.e. Supervisor	16/19
PLAYING-SESSIONS: fully illustrated	73 and 77

SILLY SYSTEM: (but not so "silly"?)	57
SLEEPERS: (particularly "Sleeping Partners")	49
SPINNING TO DISASTER?	16

SPLIT BETS: Carre }
              Cheval }
              Transversale }
              Sixainne }
	19

STAKING:	24
STAKING HIGHLIGHTED (Chapter 3)	26
STOP AT A WIN: (imprudent?)	5/64
STOP-LOSS	36/46
SUPERVISOR or "PIT BOSS"	16/19
VIDEO CAMERAS	19
WHEEL:	
specimen etc.	17
biased	21/66

=========

Other Gambling titles available from Oldcastle Books:

WIN AT GREYHOUND RACING £4.95 224pp

A comprehensive guide that shows you how to: Assess a Greyhound — Assess a Track — Read a Race — Analyse a Race — Pick winners on Form — Pick Winners on Family — Pick Winners on Fitness — Pick Winners on Class — Bet profitably.

THE EDUCATION OF A POKER PLAYER £4.95 160pp

The original classic manual of poker playing that is also a wonderful exposure of the cynical reality of the American Dream. Don't go into a game before you have read it.

WIN AT ROULETTE & WIN AT BLACKJACK — 96pp £4.95 (each)

Two excellent manuals that start you at the beginning and bring you all the way from novice to expert. Shows you the correct ways to play and how to bet sensibly and profitably.

Books from Cardoza:
Basics of Chess, Bridge, Roulette, Blackjack, Poker, Keno, Horse Racing, Craps, Slots. — Excellent introductory guides for just £1.99 each. 48pp.

Winning Casino Blackjack for the Non Counter, Casino Craps for the Winner and How to Play Winning Poker. — More advanced manuals for £3.95 each. 80pp.

Beat the Odds, 320pp, £4.95 — An encyclopedic round up, containing all the Basics series.

ORDER FORM

                Name of Book   **Price**

(1) ....

(2) ....

(3) ....

(4) ....

(5) ....

                                        Sub Total   ....

                                        15% P&P   ....

                                        Net Total   _____

Please send completed form with cheque/P.O. to Oldcastle Books, 18 Coleswood Road, Harpenden, Herts AL5 1EQ.

Name: ....

Address: ....

....

Postcode: ....

Gambling Interests: ....

....

....

THE GAMBLERS BOOK CLUB

The Gamblers Book Club offers an extensive range of titles aimed at helping you make your betting more profitable. Subjects covered include: Horse Racing, Greyhound Racing, Football, Blackjack, Roulette, Poker, Cribbage, American Football, Golf, Bingo, Backgammon and many more popular sports and casino games.

Details are absolutely FREE and include a host of special offers.

Just complete the form below or send your details to:

Dep. WAR,
The Gamblers Book Club,
18 Coleswood Road,
Harpenden,
Herts.
AL5 1EQ

Name: ....

Address: ....

....

Postcode: ....

Sports of interest: ....

....

....